GOD
BLESS
AMERICA

I had a great run

MARTIN ROSEN

God Bless America
I Had a Great Run
© Martin Rosen 2023

I have taken all steps to ensure the accuracy of the events in this memoir, but I have lived a long and full life. The dates are to the best of my 97-year-old brain's recollection. They have been fact-checked using numerous sources, including *I Have Never Forgotten You: The Life & Legacy of Simon Wiesenthal* produced by Rabbi Marvin Hier and Richard Trank, as well as *Meant to Be: A Memoir* published by The Toby Press. Still, forgive me if many of the dates and sequence of events are approximations.

DEDICATION

I wrote this book for my children, grandchildren, and for their children and grandchildren. I was no hero, but I hope you tell the story of me as someone you admire, who loved being American, who loved being Jewish, and who had a great run!

—Marty Rosen, February 21, 2023

TABLE OF CONTENTS

TABLE OF CONTENTS

INTRODUCTION

I was privileged to serve in the U.S. Army during World War II in Europe and the Pacific with basically the same outfit. When the war ended, everybody went home. Thirty or forty of us were spread across the United States, but we remained friends. I loved these men. They were different than me, but at our cores, we were the same.

One by one, they started to die. Their wives generally outlived them, so every few months, I would get a call from someone's wife saying, "John passed away this year."

In time, we were down to just two of us—me, and a buddy of mine named Bob Ronci out of Wellesley, Massachusetts.

About five years back, my wife said, "Marty, you have not heard from Bob in a while. Why don't you call him?"

Bob was one of the exceptions: He outlived his wife. Last we talked, he had sold the home and was living in a retirement home. I called the switchboard operator and asked to speak to him.

"Mr. Ronci is no longer here," she informed me.

"Can you tell me where he went?"

"I'm not legally allowed to give you that information."

"You have to tell me. We go back decades," I said, pleading with her. "We served in World War II together."

She still refused to comply. And then I thought of a question she could answer.

"Did he walk out or was he carried out?" I asked.

"I suppose I can answer that. He walked out."

I did not know how to find Bob, but I was relieved that at least he was alive.

"The next day, I received a call from a man who introduced himself as Robert Ronci, Jr.

"My father died today. He left instructions that the first person I should call was you. He has a message for you."

His message was: "God Bless America. I had a great run."

PART ONE

CHILDHOOD

I was born on September 3, 1925, the son of Irving and Kate Rosen, who lived in the Bronx. My parents were modest people, both with Jewish backgrounds. My mother was born in the United States; my father was born somewhere near the Russian-Ukrainian border, where the fighting is happening today, in 2023.

My father was a very moral and ethical man. He was a good Jew, but not a fanatic. He was an Orthodox Jew, but he did not insist that his sons be Orthodox. We did not want to be Orthodox, and he never said a word in objection.

He expected that we observed the Jewish holidays, and we respected that. If one or both of his sons chose to sit with him in synagogue on Saturday mornings, he was elated. If we did not sit with him, he was not disappointed. If he came back from synagogue and learned that we had played baseball or golf on a Saturday morning, he did not say a word.

He was a good man. I think that is the way people should be. He had a laissez-faire attitude that I should do what I wanted to do so long as I never hurt anybody in doing it.

My father came to the United States when he was fifteen or sixteen, and he brought his entire family, which included three sisters, a brother, and his mother and father. They had no money, so they lived all together in the Lower East Side part of Manhattan in New York City.

My father eventually went into the embroidery business. He owned a dress manufacturing shop in Manhattan on 7th Avenue, which is New York City's fashion district. At the height of his business, my dad had about forty people working for him. He made a modest living, but not much more than that, in part because he refused to buy and sell textiles on the Black Market.

By the time my older brother and I were born, my family had moved to the Bronx, which is one of the five boroughs of New York City. The neighborhood was primarily Jewish, but Irish and Italian as well. My mother had ten siblings, and my father had four siblings, so there were sixteen total. I had more cousins than I could count, and they all lived near me. Most lived on the same block, which had rows and rows of apartment complexes. The more affluent families lived higher up the hill on the same block—those apartments had elevators while ours did not.

Everyone thought they may have had money, but nobody had money.

It was a good bringing up. There were no complaints, no jealousy. About sixty or seventy kids lived in my apartment complex, and we all ran down the steps every day and met in the park. After all, no one owned a house big enough for six or seven people. There was no drinking or drugs or crime. We played ball and had ice cream—clean stuff.

Life was wonderful. We felt good about each other. It was a rich but poor relationship. There was no crime or fighting. Nobody owned a key. Nobody hurt anybody. Nobody took anybody else's belongings away because they had nothing to take away. If someone in the family was having a hard time, someone else very quietly gave them a bit of money. It was an easy decision: We helped our family.

It was a good life. And that is how I was brought up.

This was the late 1920s, 1930s, and the beginning of the 1940s. It was a wonderful childhood, but not significant. I broke my shoulder playing football without the proper equipment. It was a bad break, but nothing life threatening—just normal kid stuff.

Nothing crazy happened with girls. I had a large group of cousins and friends, so we went out in big groups, and everyone was gentlemanly.

But as I sit reflecting on the segments of my life, I realize in hindsight that I did have a very unusual childhood in one respect.

Me with my older brother, Leon.

Top row: Me, my brother, Leon.

Bottom row: My mom, Kate, and my dad, Irving.

FRIENDS FOR LIFE

My childhood home is located at 1925 University Avenue in the Bronx, which was then a new six-story apartment complex with 72 residential units. As I mentioned earlier, my apartment complex did not have an elevator, but up the street, where some of my mom's sisters lived, the apartment complexes were a little nicer and did have elevators.

Down the street, at 1825 University Avenue, was an elegant five-story temple, the Hebrew Institute of University Heights. I say that it was elegant because it had an elevator. The temple's rabbi was a good man: Rabbi Simon G. Kramer, who was eventually appointed by President Franklin Delano Roosevelt as an ambassador in relocating Jewish families who had escaped from a Nazi-occupied country.

Between my apartment complex and the temple were several other large apartment complexes. At that time, the Bronx was the borough that was most heavily populated with Jewish families, which meant that the children who were living in the surrounding complexes, as well as my own, went to the same synagogue. They also went to my school. I saw them in the stairwell on the way to my apartment, on the streets on my way to temple, and at the park when I went to play ball.

All in all, I had about seventy childhood friends. Seventy! We were all in the same grade, more or less. We went to dances together. We went to gym dances, meetings, and ball games together. Our bar mitzvahs were at about the same time. And later, all but a handful went to war together.

Most of us came home from that war, but two did not: My childhood friend Mike Egan was killed in Italy; and my friend Arthur Raffel was killed in France.

When the rest of us returned from war, we established a fraternal organization in their honor: The Egan Raffel Lodge of B'Nai Brith, of which I am still a member today.

For about ten years of my life—from 1940 until 1950—my childhood friends and I were all on much the same path as we turned from boys into men. Eventually, we were spread apart by geography, but we remained close throughout our lives. We attended each other's weddings and our children's bar mitzvahs. And later, we attended each other's funerals, until now, I am the only one left. Throughout our lives, we paid dues to the Egan Raffel Lodge of B'Nai Brith. Our sons and our grandsons joined. I am the only founding member still alive, and I keep paying dues, not only for Mike and Arty, but for all the men who gave me a childhood of goodness, support, and decency.

We had no great luxury other than the luxury of outlook, of ethics, and of friendship. We argued very little; the love and support was extraordinary. It is hard to imagine now that it is possible for such a large group to get along as well as we did, but we were happy for each other's successes, and delighted to see each other do well.

And the irony is that if I had lived in a more affluent neighborhood, I would not have been given this luxury.

MY FAMILY

When I was thirteen or fourteen, my brother and I decided to be partners in a paper route. We delivered a paper called *The Bronx Home News*. We loaded the papers into an old carriage and delivered them. I remember that the houses were fancy. Most of them were not even apartments but semi-detached private houses.

On Mondays, we collected payment for delivering the papers. I believe we earned a nickel or a dime per household per week, and we had to turn part of that over to the newspaper. As we were walking up the stairs to collect from one of the fancy houses, I spotted a $10 bill on the stairwell. In those days, $10 was like a million dollars to a young kid. I picked the bill up, and I thought about what my father would have told me if he was there.

He would have said: "That money doesn't belong to you."

I marched up the stairs and rang the bell.

"Does this belong to you?" I said to the lady who answered the door.

She said it did, and she took the $10. I remember thinking, *That was stupid. I didn't even ask for a reward.*

Years later, when my middle daughter, Lynn, was about thirteen or fourteen, I told her that story.

She said, "President Nixon probably wouldn't have returned that money."

I raised my children the way my parents raised me: to be honest, and not to want what doesn't belong to them. I was taught to want what belonged to me, and only what belonged to me.

My dad is honest Abe.

—Ilene Rosen Cohen, my oldest daughter

They were simple days—Great Depression days. People didn't go anywhere far. They spent time in the neighborhood. They went to church or synagogue. They took the subway to school or work, but otherwise, they were home. They rarely went on vacation. It was not an elaborate life, not glamorous like we know today, but it cultivated a good feeling among people. We did not have a television or computers or video games, and that was just fine with us. We read and listened to the radio in the evenings.

In those days, family was number one. Your love was your family. Money was number two. Vacations were number three. Cars were number four.

My first love was my family.

Family Tree

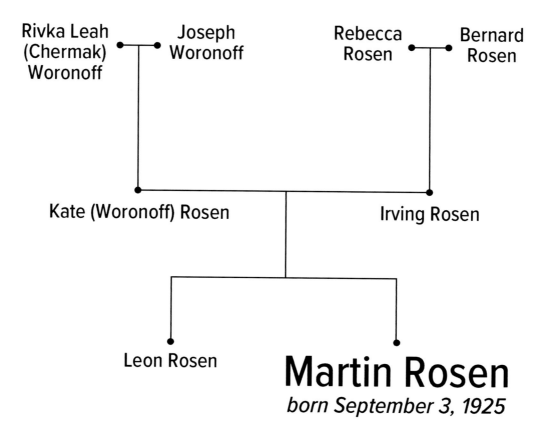

Rivka Leah (Chermak) Woronoff — Joseph Woronoff

Rebecca Rosen — Bernard Rosen

Kate (Woronoff) Rosen

Irving Rosen

Leon Rosen

Martin Rosen
born September 3, 1925

A PROMISING FUTURE

At about the same time, Simon Wiesenthal, a young man of just twenty years old, was attending the Czech Technical University in Prague. His first choice for schools had been Lwów Polytechnic, which is now Lviv Polytechnic. Either way, Simon was not admitted due to the school's cap on the number of Jews it would admit.

Simon was born in 1908, seventeen years before I was born, in what is now Ukraine, but was then Austria. His father emigrated to Austria from Russia to escape anti-Semitism and later died in combat on the Eastern Front of World War I when Simon was just seven years old.

Simon and I had very different childhoods. He faced the loss of his father and, later, his brother, who died after falling off a cliff. His entire childhood had been consumed by war and death. But his future, just like mine, was promising. Upon graduating college, Simon apprenticed as a building engineer, married his high school sweetheart, Cyla, in 1936, and built a home for his mother, stepfather, and Cyla.

A few years later, just days before the beginning of World War II, in 1939, German Foreign Minister Joachim von Ribbentrop and Soviet Foreign Minister Vyacheslav Molotov signed the Hitler-Stalin Pact, which guaranteed peace between the two countries. Behind closed doors, the pact also partitioned Soviet and German borders, defining who could control Estonia, Finland, Latvia, Lithuania, and Poland.

World War II officially began in September of 1939. Simon and his wife were living in Lwów, which was then a Polish city. On September 1, Hitler invaded Poland from the west; sixteen days later, the Soviet Union invaded from the east.

Simon Wiesenthal, his wife, and his mother were forced to give up their home, move to the Lwów Ghetto, and work in a forced labor camp. In 1941, Simon and Cyla were transferred to Janowska concentration camp, a Nazi concentration camp on the outskirts of Lwów. Cyla, who was blonde with bluish-green eyes, eventually escaped through a Polish underground organization, using forged papers that claimed she was non-Jewish. She traveled to Warsaw, where she worked for the remainder of the war in a German radio factory. Simon's mother, deemed too elderly to work, was murdered in Belzec as part of the "Final Solution."

In all, Simon lost 89 relatives during World War II.

DECEMBER 7, 1941

On December 7, 1941, I was sixteen years old. The New York Giants were playing the Washington Redskins, and we were listening to the game at my aunt's house because she had the big radio. Just before 4 p.m. Eastern Time, the broadcast was interrupted with an emergency announcement: The Imperial Japanese Navy Air Service had attacked the United States' naval base at Pearl Harbor.

I remember it like yesterday. We all asked the same question: "Where is Pearl Harbor?"

At the time, the United States was a neutral country. We were not at war yet. There was no draft. I had been living a wonderful childhood in blissful ignorance of the Pearl Harbor navy fleet located between Honolulu and Oahu in Hawaii.

I knew a little about the war consuming large portions of Europe and the Pacific. Nazi Germany had already conquered Poland, France, Belgium, and the Netherlands, annexing Austria and Czechoslovakia. They had invaded the Soviet

Union in violation of the Hitler-Stalin Pact. The Empire of Japan's expansion into China had already cost 20 million people their lives in the Pacific. A little over a year earlier—September 27, 1940—Germany, Italy, and Japan had formed an alliance in what became known as the Axis powers.

Still, large parts of America were committed to isolationism, believing that it was in America's best interest to remain neutral. Prior to the attack on Pearl Harbor, there had been no war on American soil.

Though it was technically neutral, the United States had sanctions against Japan, was aiding China, and was fighting Japan's efforts to expand into the Dutch East Indies. Beyond that, the United States had demanded that Japan withdraw from China and French Indochina.

On that day, December 7, 1941, Japan also attacked the U.S. and British military bases in the Philippines, Guam, Wake Island, Malaya, Singapore, and Hong Kong. Its goal was to send a message to the U.S. and the British Empire: Stop preventing Japanese military initiatives in the Pacific.

The next day, the United States declared war on the Empire of Japan, officially entering World War II and bringing this innocent chapter of my childhood to a close.

ENTRY INTO WORLD WAR II

In the year following the attack on Pearl Harbor, the United States military doubled in size to four million servicemen. I was still too young to serve in the military, but my childhood friends, their brothers, and my cousins enlisted or were drafted to the Armed Forces.

The rest of us continued going to school, but we lived in fear that the Japanese might bomb New York City. As a precaution against air raids, defense officials implemented blackouts, dimming the lights of New York's streets, and similar acts.

Everyone did what they could. We collected gold and silver for the war effort, and we waited for the day we could enlist. Women went to work, some for the first time, and we all rationed food and other goods.

My brother, Leon, was 15 months my senior. He was not yet eighteen, but he desperately wanted to join the war effort. The military allowed seventeen-year-olds to join, assuming their parents gave consent.

We are now in this war. We are all in it—all the way. Every single man, woman, and child is a partner in the most tremendous undertaking of our American history.

—President Franklin Roosevelt, December 9, 1941

Leon did everything he could to change my mother's mind, but my mother refused to give consent for Leon to enlist. I remember that Leon used to go into the streets and yell, "My mother is a Nazi!"

She was not a Nazi, of course, but Leon was desperate.

My mother did not back down. Under no circumstances did she want her sons to go to war.

Eventually, Leon lied, and he was able to enlist in the Air Force. He became a bombardier and flew thirty or forty bombing missions over Japan. He survived, and we had a remarkable relationship for the rest of our lives.

During most of 1942, the U.S. Navy fought again Japan in the Pacific, while the rest of the Armed Services prepared to fight Europe. I was drafted on my birthday, September 3, 1943, the same day the Allied Forces invaded Italy, and five days before Italy surrendered. I was a year ahead in high school, so by the time I was drafted, I had attended one year of college. I was ready to put my education on hold and join the war effort.

Yet, my shoulder was in terrible shape from the football injury that occurred two years earlier. As I said earlier, it was a bad break. I had been in a public hospital for a month after the accident, and I was not given the type of rehabilitation that children from richer families would have received.

When I went to register for the draft, my mother was very upset. She had two boys, and one was already in the war, so she wrote a letter explaining my injury. She thought that perhaps I would not have to go, or that I would get a soft job.

On the subway to the draft board, I took that letter, ripped it up, and threw it out.

The woman enlisting people said to me, "Boy, you don't have to go right away."

I said, "I'm ready. Let's go."

So of course, I was drafted.

When I returned home, my mother said, "What happened?"

I had never lied to my mother, and I never lied to her again, but I lied that day. I wanted to go and serve my country.

"They took me."

When my parents and I went to the draft boards to see where I was going, it was cold. It was winter, and nobody had a car, so we had to take the subway and then wait in the street, freezing, to learn where we were being sent.

The loyalty, family love, and support were extraordinary. And what I remember carefully right now, as I am older, is that all the fathers went with their sons.

PART TWO

THE 100TH INFANTRY DIVISION

was first sent to Camp Upton in Long Island to be inducted. I remember that it was very cold, and I took test after test. The government had decided that to win the war, they needed students: They didn't need soldiers. They gave all enlisted men an intelligence test, and they sent those who scored well to Fort Benning in Georgia, where the plan was to then send them to administer the war in Japan and Germany, which the United States military anticipated winning earlier than it did.

Most of my childhood friends scored well on those tests because we had been raised in a clean environment where we had been expected to study hard and prioritize education. I also scored well, so along with many of my friends, I was sent to Fort Benning, Georgia, for basic training.

It was tough because we were soft kids. Growing up, my mother made the bed for me. And here I was digging red clay and getting the dirt beat out of me. The good news, at least for my mother, was this: Even though I wanted to be a soldier, I was eventually going to land an Army office job.

But halfway through the sixteen weeks of basic training, some geniuses in Washington said, "We may lose the war. We need to teach these kids to fight."

Washington abolished the program I was in, and every program like it. Instead, we were sent into basic infantries. The U.S. military was getting ready for Operation Neptune, better known as D-Day, where a lot of the soldiers who could have otherwise been given better military jobs ended up dying on the beaches of Normandy.

In December 1943, I was sent to the 100th Infantry Division, which was a ranger division operating from Fort Bragg in North Carolina. It was tough as hell, but we were young and athletic, so we could do it. We had 100 days to complete the rest of training, and that would take us right up to D-Day.

D-Day was on June 6, 1944. On a Saturday night late in May, I got a call that the first sergeant wanted to see me.

"I am transferring you out of this outfit," he told me.

"Why?" I asked.

"We are over T-O," which is Army lingo for, "We have too many men." Divisions had to have a certain number of men, but the sergeant explained that we had six too many.

I was a kid, and I was stupid, so instead of being happy that I was getting out of infantry, I said, "But I am happy here. My buddies are all here."

I remember the sergeant said to me, "We picked six men at random. You are going to Camp Gruber in Muskogee, Oklahoma."

I was a little sad.

When I passed the office, I looked at the bulletin board and saw the names of the other five men being transferred. They were all Jewish. This was the 1940s, and America was aloof from any type of understanding of what minorities were. Most of the Army consisted of people who had never met a Jew, and the feeling was that Gentiles would be more comfortable if their divisions did not include any Jews. I guess that we were considered slackers and physically lazy.

There was a lot of anti-Semitism. I suppose the first sergeant wanted to purge the infantry of the Jews. He never made it clear, but maybe he figured they would be better fighters without us. He said it was random, but there were six Jews, and the six of us were sent to a combat engineer battalion.

He was probably a bigot, but he probably saved our lives.

AWOL

By the end of 1944, the Allies had successfully pushed back the war in Europe. Soviet troops had liberated Kiev. Mussolini had been deposed, though a puppet Fascist regime was in place when the Germans seized control of Rome and northern Italy. In due time, the Allies liberated Rome, almost all of France, as well as most of Belgium and a portion of the southern Netherlands.

The United States Army was getting ready to deploy mass numbers of men to Europe to finish off the war. It looked to me as though they were moving all remaining troops to make one final push against the Germans. At the same time, and unbeknownst to us, of course, the Germans were planning the Battle of the Bulge, which was World War II's last major German offensive effort of the Western Front. In the end, it was the bloodiest battle fought by the United States in World War II, with at least 8,400 Americans killed. Despite the large number of deaths, the Allies won, with the Nazis suffering 100,000 casualties.

I was fortunate that I would not be going directly into battle. Instead, I would be sent from Camp Gruber in Muskogee, Oklahoma, to Camp Myles Standish in Taunton, Massachusetts. Camp Myles Standish is where soldiers went before and after being sent overseas through the Boston Port of Embarkment. We would be headed to England to build Bailey Bridges. (More on that later.)

The soldiers in my unit generally fell into two camps: young men like me who had recently been sent into the combat engineer battalion from the 100th Infantry Division, and soldiers who had been in the Army for years. Some of us of us were eighteen- and nineteen-year-olds, and the rest were thirty-year-olds. While several of the older men went to bars, the young soldiers like me never broke the rules. When we were on furlough, we went to dinners and the movies.

But on the Sunday of Thanksgiving weekend, 1944, just before I was deployed, I committed a crime.

We had all been given a one-day furlough before being deployed overseas. Still, it was illegal to leave the camp without "leave," which required a pass for departure. The term for the crime was and is "AWOL," which stands for absent without leave. Soldiers who went AWOL could be prosecuted and punished.

You have to understand that these were very emotional days because we were playing for a serious prize: life. None of us had experienced anything like this before. I was barely eighteen years old, and I was leaving for good, with no idea as to whether I was coming back.

With great trepidation, a group of us broke into the barracks, and we typed out a phony pass so that we could leave.

Our plan was not to run away for one day. We wanted to say goodbye to our families.

I, along with an Irishman named O'Connell, boarded an early morning train from Massachusetts to New York. When I arrived in New York, I caught a bus to Penn Station, and eventually made my way home. I told my parents that I did not know where I was going, but as soon as I found out, I would send them a letter that would end with:

- "Regards to Ethel" if I was going to England.
- "Regards to Frank" if I was going to France.
- "Regards to Geraldine" if I was going to Germany.

There was a saying in those days: Loose lips sink ships. If people knew where our military boats were headed, the enemy could more easily attack our vessels. Under no circumstances was I supposed to tell my parents where I was going. But like I said, these were emotional times. My parents already had one son serving overseas. Not knowing was worse than knowing.

I remember being on the train home at night. O'Connell was with me, and the train was filled with young, pretty women traveling from college to visit their families for Thanksgiving. They flirted with us easily, knowing that we had no future. We were going to war, and they were headed back to college.

When I returned to base on Sunday night at about 10 p.m., I had a cold, so I headed to the medic, where I ran into my first sergeant.

"If you stayed away from going to big cities without a pass, you would not have gotten sick," he said.

"It's nice of you to be concerned for my health," I said. "But how did you know that I was there … unless you were there, too?"

Technically, what I had done was a crime, but fortunately, I wasn't the only guy who did it, and nothing bad came out of it—other than that cold.

A few days later, we packed and marched with our belongings into town to load onto a boat. I remember that older women had gathered on the pier to say goodbye and to send the soldiers with coffee, cakes, and donuts. By now, I knew that I was headed to northeastern Europe, so I quickly wrote a note for my mother, ending with: "Regards to Ethel." I handed that note to one of the many kind women who were seeing us off.

For years, I wondered if that letter made its way to my mother. When I returned from the war, I learned that it never did. The woman I handed it to knew that loose lips sink ships. Writing the letter was a crime—my second in just a few days—and sending it would have been a crime.

The day was December 1, 1944. It was the last time, and the only time, that I broke the rules.

THE COMBAT ENGINEER BATTALION

T he difference between infantry and combat engineers is not too distinct. Infantries are foot soldiers; combat engineers are the foot soldiers who know how to dig up mines and set booby traps on bridges. When foot soldiers went from the United States to Europe during that time of the war, they bypassed England and went directly to France or Germany. My original outfit, the 100th Infantry Division, for instance, spent 163 days in combat during World War II. It drove against the German Winter Line, took Bertichamps and Clairupt, and seized Raon-l'Étape and Saint-Blaise-Moyenmoutier. The 100th Infantry Division was also responsible for the fall of Bitche.

Before that, the 100th Infantry Division fought in the Nazi-initiated Battle of the Bulge, which began on December 16, 1944, the same day the combat engineers, including me and the five other Jews in my outfit, arrived in England. We had left through the Boston Port of Embarkation and eventually were stationed in Wallingford, England, on the River Thames to learn how to build Bailey bridges.

U.S. soldiers from the 100th Infantry Division

Killed in action:	**883**
Wounded in action:	**3,539**
Missing in action:	**483**
Prisoners of war:	**491**
Total battle casualties:	**5,083**

Source: Army Battle Casualties and Nonbattle Deaths in World War II, Final Report (Statistical and Accounting Branch Office of the Adjutant General, 1 June 1953)

The Bailey bridge was invented in 1941 by Donald Bailey, an English civil engineer. It was so important that the senior British Army officer Bernard Law Montgomery once said, "Without the Bailey bridge, we should not have won the war."

In short, a Bailey bridge is strong enough for a tank to cross over it, but it is portable, light, and can be lifted into place without a crane. The Bailey bridge was the only thing that allowed the Allied forces to cross the English Channel and travel from England into France.

Instead of fighting in the Battle of the Bulge, combat engineers were trained in England to build and operate Bailey bridges. And this is how that bigot from Birmingham, Alabama, saved my life.

As a combat engineer, it helps to be a big guy. I was only 144 pounds, but I did what I had to. I never slacked off, and I stayed with the outfit for most of my time in the war. I ended up loving the other soldiers, none of whom were like me. About ten or twelve of us were eighteen-year-old kids, and the rest were men who had been drafted in their early thirties. They were from Coast Artillery, which means they had been guarding the Atlantic Coast and looking out for spies. Their outfit was abolished, and the military merged the soldiers from Coast Artillery in with my outfit, along with a mismatch of other kids. We were an amazingly homogeneous bunch of men in that we were all as different as could be.

There was a lot of prejudice, on both sides. Some of it was unpleasant; some of it was pugilistic because I refused to let people call me dirty things.

But it went both ways. Keep in mind that a person's religion in those times was far more important than religion is now. There was more dissent around religion. Our dog tags were even stamped with our religion: "P" for Protestant, "C" for Catholic, and "H" for Jewish. I counted heads, and they counted heads.

If someone's last name was O'Brien, I assumed he was a drunk. If someone was Protestant, I assumed he was an uneducated hillbilly. When I met somebody Irish, Black, or whatever, I did not like him because I thought I knew who he was. I didn't know who he was.

I had been raised in the Bronx, so almost everyone I knew was Jewish. The most anti-Semitism I was ever exposed to at that point was when I served in the United States military while fighting against Nazi Germany.

Eventually, the camaraderie broke the prejudice.

They used to joke, "Hey, Rosen. You are a Jew, but you are not a bad guy."

I would say, "Why would I be a bad guy?"

And the joke would continue: "I would even let you marry my sister," to which I would respond, "Who the hell wants to marry your sister?"

I spent almost all my war years with this same group of men, starting in the United States, and going to England, Germany, and then France and the Philippine Islands. At one point, we were on a ship together for sixty days. (I will tell you about that in a bit.) We would sleep on the deck because it was so hot. We would look up at the stars and talk about where we would be in twenty years.

I remember one soldier saying he would not make it out of the war, and another guy saying he would live to be ninety.

I said, "I will be happy to live to fifty." I was just a young kid at that time—nineteen. I thought that fifty would be a good compromise.

I stayed in touch with those who survived for the rest of my life. One by one, they have all died up to now.

I believe I am the only member still alive.

Me, as a young man during my Army years.

SHOVELING BODIES IN SCHÖNECKEN

The soldiers in my outfit did a good job, so we stayed in England for a while building bridges. In April of 1945, it was time for us to transfer to what was soon to become my least favorite place on earth, Schönecken, Germany. When we arrived in Schönecken, we did absolutely nothing. While the war in the Pacific raged on, the war on the Eastern Front in Europe was over in most places but not all.

Hitler had not yet committed suicide, but most of the Nazi soldiers were done fighting. In due time, on April 30, Hitler killed himself. Seven days later, May 7, 1945, Germany surrendered.

We celebrated, but remember that the war was not over in the Pacific. We were still fighting the Japanese, so we stayed in Schönecken, waiting orders. At the time, the town consisted of women, boys under the age of fifteen, men over sixty-five, and many, many dead bodies of both Allied and Axis soldiers.

My first sergeant was a bit of a bigot who would pick on me for being

Jewish, but I could handle it. Two days after the war ended, he called me into the office and said, "You and another man are going to go looking for dead American bodies."

The Germans had piled bodies together in forests. When the war ended, the first thing my company wanted to do was retrieve the American bodies and give them a respectful burial at Luxembourg American Cemetery, where General Patton was buried.

The war had been over for just 48 hours when I was given this assignment. The last shots had not yet been fired, so I carried a submachine gun while the other soldier drove the truck through Schönecken to the office of the *bürgermeister*, the mayor.

"Round up all of your able-bodied men between sixteen and sixty-two," said the other soldier who had been assigned this horrific job. "Tell them to bring a shovel."

For two days—May 9 and May 10 of 1945—we took American bodies out of the forest graves, loaded them into the truck, and drove them back to Luxembourg.

An American soldier wears a dog tag with two identical tags on it. My job was to untwine the two tags, put one in a bag with the dead soldier's personal belongings, which I searched to find, and tie that bag around his ankle. The other tag I kept around his neck so he could be buried with the proper burial: P for a Protestant burial, H for a Jewish burial, and C for a Catholic burial.

I will never forget the first day we left Schönecken with dead bodies in the back of our truck. We drove back to Luxembourg at about six or seven o'clock. It was getting dark. When we arrived, we saw hundreds of soldiers taking care of thousands of bodies.

The other soldier with me that day was a kid just like me. He looked at me and said, "What are we going to do? How are we going to get these bodies off the truck and into a proper burial?"

Another soldier, who was much older, took one look at us and said, "You guys go get a cup of coffee."

We watched as two soldiers stood behind the truck and two others jumped in the back of the truck with the bodies. They started tossing the cadavers off like cardboard boxes.

Two days. We did that for two days.

After two days, we said to the colonel: "We cannot do this assignment."

Some other soldiers could do it, but I could not. I saw more dead bodies during those two days than a person who works in a funeral parlor sees in a lifetime. I was just a kid—nineteen at the time.

But that was part of what it took to be American Jew fighting against the Nazis. I still remember every detail of it.

FURLOUGH IN MARSEILLE

A s you know, on May 7, 1945, Germany surrendered its armed forces to the Allies, marking the end of World War II on the Eastern Front in Europe. President Roosevelt had died just a month earlier, on April 12, which meant that the vice president, a great man by the name of Harry Truman, assumed the presidency.

The United States was still at war with Japan. And unlike the war in Europe, the war in the Pacific was not primarily a land war. It was a naval war that required jumping from island to island. Unbeknownst to us, President Truman decided to split the invasions of Japan into two parts. The first would get control of the Philippine Islands and use it as a jumping off point to invade the southern island of Kyushu. Part two would be an invasion that would start in the United States and join forces with the troops invading Kyushu.

The troops invading from the United States would first be sent home on furlough.

They were the lucky ones. The second part of President Truman's plan did not materialize, and those men were released from duty. My unit was not so lucky. We were part of the first group, which was to head to Kyushu.

After we finished our service in Schönecken, we were transferred by train to Camp Victorette in Marseille, France, which was a staging point for Allied forces to go to Japan. The winter of 1944 had been one of the worst winters Europe had ever seen, so while serving on the European Front, we were outfitted with heavy winter gear. At Camp Victorette, we prepared for war in the Pacific by changing to lighter clothes, trading our rifles for bayonets, and learning about the Japanese culture, mind, and way of life.

Me in Marseille.

In Marseille, I was given a furlough. It had been freezing cold in Germany—so cold that most of us did not shower for three months. Being on furlough in the French Riviera felt glamorous. I had a bed, a warm shower, and three meals a day, served by a waitress. It was extraordinary.

During my furlough, I spent most of my spare time at the temple because I did not have any money or desire to frequent the bars. While I was there, I spotted three soldiers, in Russian uniform.[1]

If you know your history, you know that the then-Soviet Union lost twenty million people, the highest number of deaths experienced by a country in World War II. Twenty million! You also know that the war was complex for the Soviets. The Soviets signed the non-aggression pact with Nazi Germany a week before World War II began, which allowed both the Nazis and the Soviets to invade Poland. But Germany later invaded the Soviet Union. In 1941, the Soviets joined the Allies. Soviet dictator Joseph Stalin became one of the "Big Three," the term given to then-U.S. President Franklin Roosevelt, British Prime Minister Winston Churchill, and Stalin to describe the leaders of the most powerful countries comprised of the Allied Forces.

I remember thinking that those three Russian soldiers were men whose brothers and friends and cousins were dying, all around them. Their country was in turmoil. Though the United States saw no combat on its mainland, Russia had been invaded, and it had been invaded by the very country that it signed a pact with. Remember, too, that I met these gentlemen in a temple. Not only were they Russian, but they were Jews.

I spent the week with them, eating dinner, and trying to communicate. Though we did not speak the same language, we knew each other's thoughts. The camaraderie that we felt was a little mind-boggling now, as I think back on it.

---

1   The Union of Soviet Socialist Republics (USSR) was a federation that included fifteen "socialist republics," including Russia. It was run by the Communist Party and was dissolved in 1991. Though calling the country Russia was not technically correct, in common vernacular, the USSR, Russia, and the Soviet Union were used synonymously.

Growing up, I had played ball with Irish and Italian boys. We called each other names, but it was the kind of big talk that happens in sports. They called me dirty. I called them drunks. It was nothing that we could not take.

I did not realize how much anti-Semitism existed until the war. The extent of it was staggering. When I was sixteen and just helping with the war effort, we would read in the papers about what was happening with the mass graves. The papers did not tell us everything. They left most things out. Occasionally, we would see pictures, and we would think, "This cannot be true."

I lived in a modest but kind place. My mother never even gave me a key to my apartment because no one would have thought of breaking in or hurting us.

But I saw what was happening in Germany. I shoveled the dead bodies. Those Russian Jews saw it too, and we did not have to speak the same language to know the same thing: to be Jewish was a frightening thing.

At one point, years later, I was lecturing at a high school about my time in the war, and later, my time working with Simon Wiesenthal. I remember a big kid standing up in that high-school auditorium and saying, "I think the Jews got what they deserved. They deserved to be killed because they did not fight back."

Everyone was quiet. They wanted to know what I would say.

He was a big kid—about six feet tall—and I called him to the podium.

"What is your name?" I asked.

"Rasmus."

"Rasmus, you are now James, and you live in Warsaw. Your mother and father have been taken by the Nazis, who come to your house. They tell you, your little sister, and your grandmother that you have two minutes to gather your personal belongings. The Nazis put you, your little sister, and your grandmother in a truck—a crowded truck where you barely have room to sit down. Your grandfather? They have already killed him.

"You are in that truck for four days. You urinate in your pants, and you defecate in your pants. Your grandmother dies along the way, but her body remains in the truck with you and your little sister, who has been crying the entire time.

"The Nazis open the door, and they start sorting people—some to the left, some to the right. They throw the dead bodies, like cardboard boxes into a pile. Your grandmother lands on top of the body of a dead child. You can see her face before it is concealed by another dead body.

"Tell me, James. Would you fight back?"

Rasmus started to cry. He didn't need to give any answers.

When we think about the people who died in the war, we think of the six million Jews, but more than six million people died in the Holocaust. Gays, Jehovah's Witnesses, Romani and Sinti, Poles, Blacks, and the disabled were also rounded up and killed by the Nazis. Maybe eleven million people were killed in the Holocaust. How many were killed by the Empire of Japan? We know that twenty million people were killed in the Russian front alone. Maybe fifty or seventy-five million or even one hundred million people were killed in World War II. It's incredible.

And someone had to kill them! When we throw around these numbers—six million Jews, eleven million in the Holocaust, seventy-five million total in the entire war—the number we do not know is this: How many people were killing? Because someone had to be doing the killing. After a while, it seemed that they enjoyed killing. They would beat people up before putting them in the ovens. They didn't have to do that. They stole our goods, they raped our wives and sisters, and they robbed everyone. And then they killed them while laughing.

The things they did were beyond belief. How do you turn thousands or maybe millions of people into animals? How could this have happened? How do you fight this kind of evil? How do you even try? Those numbers are mind-boggling.

Those Russian Jews and I knew the same thing: God went on vacation. What was happening could not have otherwise happened.

THE LIST

On the banks of the Danube River in Upper Austria lies the town of Mauthausen. Above it sits a hill that was the location of a concentration camp by the same name. All concentration camps were evil; Mauthausen was one of the worst. The site was chosen because of its granite quarry. Prior to the war, granite from the quarry had been used to pave the streets of Vienna.

Hitler had a different plan for the granite. He would use it to realize his vision for reconstructing Germany's architecture. Prisoners in Mauthausen were essential to his plan of collecting the granite.

The men and women, mostly Jewish, at Mauthausen were forced to carry boulders, sometimes weighing more than 100 pounds, to the top of the quarry using a 186-step stone staircase known as the "Stairs of Death." Many, many Holocaust victims died on that staircase. They were starving and exhausted, and they simply collapsed.

In 1943, Heinrich Himmler, who was the main architect of the Holocaust, visited Mauthausen. The commander of Mauthausen at that time was an animal named Franz Ziereis. To entertain Himmler, Ziereis organized for 1,000 Jewish victims to assemble on the rim of the granite quarry, where SS officials pushed them, one by one, to fall 165 feet to their deaths.[2]

This became known as a game. It was called the Parachute Jump.

More than 135,000 prisoners were murdered at Mauthausen—beaten, shot, worked to death, starved, or pushed off a cliff as part of a sick game. The Parachute Jump was one of the favorite pastimes of the men who ran Mauthausen. They enjoyed it. They laughed as they the skeletal bodies of Holocaust victims fall to the pit of the quarry.

Simon Wiesenthal had been held prisoner by Nazis in a number of concentration camps by the time he arrived in Mauthausen. He had escaped death more than once. At times, his life was spared because he was considered vital as an architect. At other times, he got lucky. He once was kneeling while a Nazi shot a line of Jewish men. When the Nazi got to Simon, he was out of bullets. Another time, Simon was spared death because he was needed to paint a sign.

Simon arrived in Mauthausen in February of 1945. If the United States Army had not liberated the camp on May 5, 1945, it is hard to imagine that he would have survived much longer. Simon was a big man. Before the war, and when I met him years after the war, he weighed about 220 pounds. But on that day, just three days before the complete surrender of Germany, Simon weighed 89 pounds, one for each of the 89 relatives of his that had been killed. Other than blades of grass, he had not eaten in five days.

Simon would later be reunited with Cyla, and they would have a kind and loving daughter, Paulinka, who would in turn marry a lovely Dutchman and give Simon and Cyla grandchildren.

But on May 5, Simon believed that everybody he knew and loved had been murdered.

---

2   The *Schutzstaffel*, or SS, were the leaders of Nazi military and police forces, overseeing concentration camps, ethnic identity, and intelligence, among other atrocities. In their minds, they were the "racial elite." In reality, they were the worst of the animals.

The Americans had designated a Polish man named Kazimierz Rusinek as the man in charge of providing former prisoners with the paperwork that would allow them to leave Mauthausen. When Simon asked Rusinek for a permit, Rusinek responded with, "What do you want from me, Musselman?[3] If the Nazis had been around two more days, you would have left through the chimney."

Instead of giving Simon a permit, Rusinek, who went on to become a propagandist for Communist Poland, beat 89-pound Simon Wiesenthal.

This beating changed the course of Simon's life and legacy. On the way to the office of the U.S. Commanding Officer to file a formal complaint against Rusinek, Simon walked by a group of SS men who were shackled and being interrogated by the U.S. Army in front of prisoners. This, for Simon, was a shadow of justice.

Simon asked if he could stay to help. Every few days, a Nazi would come out of the hills, and the Americans would capture him. Simon was more than happy to sit alongside the Americans and translate as they held the Nazis accountable. Eventually, U.S. soldiers asked Simon to write a list of the Nazis who had tortured him while he was held prisoner in Auschwitz, Płaszów, Gross-Rosen, Janowska, Buchenwald, and Mauthausen.

Simon's list included ninety-one Nazi war criminals. It was his own personal list of the war criminals he encountered. He listed names, ranks, specific dates, and detailed recollections of the war crimes he witnessed during his nearly six years of being a prisoner. On that list was Friedrich Katzmann, the SS official responsible for designing "The Solution of the Jewish Question in the District of Galicia," a sixty-two-page report detailing the extermination of Jews which was used as evidence in the Nuremberg Trials. For the most part, though, it was not a major list. Remember, he was just a guy. He was an architect. He was nobody different from you or me.

---

3   *Musselman* was a term referring to prisoners on the way to gas chambers.

ABOARD THE LURLINE

The Lurline was a luxury ocean liner that a private shipping and navigation company built for voyages from America to Hawaii and Australia. When the Japanese bombed Pearl Harbor, the Lurline was carrying 765 passengers from Honolulu to San Francisco. The Lurline made the second leg of its journey under radio silence at night to avoid Japanese attacks.

Shortly thereafter, upon the United States entering into the war, the Lurline became a troop ship, having been purchased as part of the government's War Shipping Administration.

My outfit boarded the Lurline in mid-June of 1945 to eventually make our way to the Philippine Islands. The short way from Marseille to the Philippines would have been from the Mediterranean Sea through the Suez Canal to the Red Sea and into the Indian Ocean.

We took the long route. We were unable to go the short route because we knew the Japanese submarines would be looking for us, waiting for a chance to bomb our troop ships. Instead, from Marseille into the Gulf of Lion, we then traveled through the Mediterranean Sea to the Strait of Gibraltar and west into the Panama Canal out to the Pacific Coast, Pearl Harbor, and then to Manila in the Philippines, where we were to invade the island of Kyushu.

It was a long trip for Army sailors. Navy soldiers are accustomed to long stretches of time at sea, but we were not. The trip took about five or six weeks and was exceedingly hot. None of the Army men knew what to do with themselves aboard that boat, so we became a little stir crazy. Occasionally we washed down the deck, but for the most part, we had no work to do. As long as we were behaving, we were left alone.

The Lurline was six-bunks high, and a lot of us slept on the top deck under the stars because it was cooler, though not cool enough to be comfortable.

My first job out of college was in investment banking. One day, I was lamenting the fact that I was working around the clock. My grandfather said to me, "When I was nineteen, I was on a boat to Japan to fight in World War II. What you are doing is nothing."

He put it all in perspective. Our family is so much better for all the life lessons that my grandfather has taught us.

—Andrew Cohen, my oldest grandson

We arrived at Balboa in the Panama Canal on August 1, and we were all granted a one-night furlough. All of us—the entire ship with hundreds of soldiers. Let me repeat that: The entire ship was on furlough. I had never, and have never since, heard of such a thing, but that is what happened on August 1, 1945, in the Panama Canal. I suppose the officers figured that we were all getting the short end of the stick by having to travel straight from the European Front to join the Pacific Front.

Four soldiers never returned from their furloughs. I have always wondered what happened to those four men. Did they attempt to run? Were they shot in the back? Are they still alive, out there somewhere in Panama, as 97-year-old men? Were they arrested and sent to jail?

I have no idea. If I'm being honest, I thought that more would have gone AWOL, but most of us returned to the Lurline.

After spending the night in Balboa, we moved on to the Western side of the Panama Canal and traveled toward Pearl Harbor.

A few days later, on August 6, 1945, President Truman dropped an atomic bomb on Hiroshima, which is a capital of one of the prefectures of Japan. (A prefecture is a similar concept as a state.) This was the first time in history a nuclear weapon had been used, and the city was destroyed.

Still, the Japanese wanted to keep their empire and refused an unconditional surrender. Despite several days of negotiations, they did not surrender.

Three days later, on August 9, 1945, President Truman dropped another bomb, this time on Nagasaki, which was located on the southern Island of Kyushu.

At that moment, we were on the Lurline, a few days away from Pearl Harbor. By now, we knew that Pearl Harbor was an American naval base.

The captain said, "Now hear this! Now hear this! The war is over."

We went crazy with cheers. We hoped that we would return to Pearl Harbor and then be sent home.

"However, our orders are to keep going."

Me (left) with Leon.

MY BROTHER IN MANILA

Eventually, the Lurline made its way to the Philippines, landing in Manila. We were transferred to the Chinese Cemetery. Earlier in the war, Japan had executed and buried at the Chinese Cemetery the many brave Filipinos who resisted the Japanese occupation. By the time we arrived, the Chinese Cemetery was being used by Allied troops.

Throughout the war, I had done my best to keep in touch with my parents and my brother, but correspondences were slow. I knew that Leon had been on approximately thirty missions flying B-29s in Guam and Tinian. He knew that I had been in Germany at the end of the European War. Then, we lost touch. I assumed he was still in the Guam/Tinian area; he assumed I was in Germany.

A good buddy of mine who was serving with my brother spotted a picture of me in the *Stars and Stripes*, a military newspaper. He called my brother and said, "Marty is in the Philippines."

What I didn't know was that Leon was also in Manila. I had lost track of him, but somehow, in this great big world, he and I both ended up in Manila at the same time.

You can imagine my joy when I happened to spot him in a bar one night. Isn't that incredible? I hadn't seen Leon in two years, and we happen to stumble into each other in a bar in Manila.

By this time, Leon was an officer, and the Army had strict rules about relationships between enlisted soldiers and officers. We weren't allowed to meet in the Army barracks, so we saw each other in parks and restaurants. We didn't get to see each other as often as we would have liked, but it was enough. I was starting to feel as if God was returning from his vacation, and that I would make it out of the war in one piece—and that my brother, who had to spend an extra year in the Army because he was an officer, would also make it home.

But not quite yet.

Grandfather was an amazing brother.
He took care of my uncle; he always wanted
what was best for him.

—Bari Cohen Klein, my granddaughter

BATAAN

In due time, soldiers were sent home based on their length of service. I was drafted upon my eighteenth birthday, and most of my outfit consisted of men in their thirties. I was one of the youngest men around, which meant it was not my time to go home.

One by one, my outfit broke up as the soldiers returned to their families in the United States. I stayed.

At the time, the U.S. Army had a small group of engineers in Bataan in need of a radio operator. Someone looked at my service record and saw that I knew how to operate a radio, so I was sent to the Province of Bataan in the Central Luzon region of the Philippines. This is the same Bataan where three years earlier, American and Filipino prisoners of war were marched sixty-five miles to various prison camps. This became known as the Bataan Death March due to the torture and mass killings of soldiers by the Japanese.

I was not in the Bataan Death March, but I was in *that* Bataan. I lived in that jungle.

I was sent with one other White man and no Jewish men. Everyone else was Black. Let me back up here and say this: When most people think of World War II, they think that anti-Semitism was a problem in Germany. They fail to understand how big of a problem anti-Semitism was in the United States (and everywhere in the world) at that time. The history books paint it as a German problem, but outside of the cocoon of my childhood in the Bronx, anti-Semitism was—and still is—everywhere. The war taught me that.

It was a contentious time, and like I said earlier, we were all counting heads. In fact, the Army was segregated during World War II. It was not until the Korean war in 1950, when the Army had a hard time filling all-White units, that the U.S. Army integrated. Even then, it was for reasons of military efficiency and power, not for reasons of principle and justice.

Soon after arriving in Bataan, the only other White man was sent home.

No one was mean or nasty to me in Bataan, but I was not supposed to be there. I didn't belong. I was in an all-Black unit as a White Jewish man. From the time I woke up, no one spoke to me. I was in a bloody hot jungle, and no one other than the men I was with knew I was there. I had never even received a paycheck.

Eventually, I said to myself, "I am never going to get out of here."

I bummed a 23-mile ride across the Manila Bay on a Navy boat. When I arrived in Manila, the colonel was very annoyed with me.

I said, "I am over in Lemay, Bataan, and I am thinking of going over the hill," army lingo for running away.

The colonel said, "Why the hell would you do that? The war is over, stupid."

"Not for me, Sir."

"That's even more stupid. What does that mean?"

"Well, Sir, I'm the only White soldier in Bataan. No one speaks to me. I'm not getting mail. The only people who are here do not care what happens to me."

He said, "I understand your problem. I'm from Birmingham, Alabama."

He was probably a White bigot, though he did not say he was. Instead, he said, "What did you do before the war?"

"Nothing," I said.

"That's even further stupid. You had to do something."

"I went to college for a year," I said.

When he found out that I had taken college courses in accounting, he transferred me out. I went back to Manila, and three or four weeks later, I went home.

That was the end of my Army career. I went to some interesting places and had some unique experiences. The Army made a man out of a boy. None of my future successes would have been possible without the experience I had in the Army.

I have never heard of another World War II soldier who served in the European war, the Pacific war, and the Philippines, including Bataan. I do not know this for a fact, but I suspect I am the only one. But let's keep things in perspective: I was no war hero.

PART THREE

MY EDUCATION

When I returned to New York after serving in World War II, I was 20 years old. The American government had programs to help GIs returning from war to attend school, but I decided I did not want to go back to school for a few months.

I wanted to do two things: chase girls and play ball.

A buddy of mine was a counselor in a camp. He asked if I would like to go, and I figured that was as good of a chance as any to play ball and chase girls, so I said I would. I did that for the summer.

After Labor Day, I had a meeting with myself. It was September 3, 1946, so I was exactly twenty-one years old. I said, "Now it's time to go to work."

Prior to the war, I had attended City College, which was the Harvard of America for Jewish boys. I could have transferred to Harvard for free thanks to the GI programs, but my credits from City College would not have transferred, so I would have lost a year. And I was hungry for success.

I went back to City College, and I studied accounting, as did almost every Jewish boy, because we knew we could get a college degree without going to graduate school. While I was in accounting school, an interesting case was making its way through the courts. A certified public accountant from New York City with the last name Bercu had been consulted on a complicated tax case after an attorney told his client that they would not legally be able to make a certain tax deduction. Bercu reviewed the case, and his opinion was that it could be deducted.

Bercu submitted a bill for his work. When the client did not pay the bill, Bercu sued in municipal court. The case was dismissed on the ground that it constituted unlicensed practice of law.

I decided I wanted to be a tax lawyer.

At the time, I was single, and the United States government was paying for my education, so I registered for New York University's law school, which was the third or fourth finest law school in the nation. My post-Army education took me six years to complete, but eventually, I earned a juris doctorate and a master's of law in taxation.

While I was in law school, I was also working as a CPA, and then as a treasury agent, so those years were grueling. But remember, I had shoveled the dead American bodies, so I could handle it. I woke up at five o'clock, took the Bronx subway downtown, worked at my job, and then I ate a sandwich before going to the law school. On the subway ride home, I did my homework. Sometimes, the subway was crowded, so I stood on the train, holding my fat legal book. When I arrived home at midnight, I had an hour or two of homework left. I got a few hours of sleep, and then I woke up the next day and did the same thing.

By the time my education was complete, I was 27 years old. I had experience as a CPA and a U.S. treasury agent. Plus, I earned my juris doctor and a master's in law in taxation.

I had all the guns and education behind me to become a successful tax lawyer accountant.

TREASURY AGENT TO WALL STREET

On December 31, 1949, I was 24 years old. I had finished college, and I was in the middle of law school at night. By day, I was a CPA, and I was making peanuts, which did not bother me. What did bother me was the lack of challenges in my professional career. I was bored. I disliked adding numbers. I wanted work that made me think.

I could not get a job at the major firms that offered more challenging work for two reasons, the first being that I was Jewish. Major firms did not hire Jewish men in those days. The second reason was that I attended law school five out of seven nights. The major firms wanted people who would stay put, and they knew I had more ambition than to be an accountant at a big firm.

I had a mediocre job at a mediocre firm.

A pal of mine told me that the U.S. Treasury Department was going to hire 135 new treasury agents in the New York area. Even though I knew very little about the Treasury Department, I submitted my application with the Civil Service Department to become a Treasury agent.

I received in the mail a notice that the Treasury agent exam was the same day the Certified Public Accountant exam. I decided that I would not sit for the Treasury exam because the CPA exam was more important. If I had kept that decision, my life would have been changed materially.

I forgot to tell you that I had balls back in those days. In due time, I came to a new decision. I called the Civil Service Department and told them they booked the exam for the wrong day because an applicant who wanted to become both a Treasury agent and a CPA would have to decide between the two. The woman on the phone told me that I was not the only one with this problem.

A few days later, I received a letter from the Civil Service Department announcing a second test date for everyone who was also taking the CPA exam.

I remember that the test was on a Saturday morning. On Friday night, I had a poker game with a bunch of friends. We finished at four o'clock in the morning.

"You guys go to bed," I told my friends. "I am taking the exam."

Marty is a man's man. He plays golf, gambles, and smokes cigars.

And then there is this other side of him, as a professional, as a mayor, as a philanthropist. Even now, at 97 years old, what he does is incredible. He is suffering fatigue from radiation, and he is still helping people when they call him for advice.

—Larry Cohen, our son-in-law

I figured I would give it a try, and if I didn't pass, I could wait for another try.

I finished number one out of approximately 1,000 applicants that day, so I got a job at the Treasury Department and started on January 9, 1950. I had been making $5,500 a year, and at the Treasury Department, I was making $7,500. I was lucky because I had the best boss in the entire IRS. He took a liking to me and treated me a bit like his son. I joined his squad, and he was a wonderful leader.

My job at the Treasury Department was the best job of my professional career, and it was a big change from my previous job. It was challenging. I was handed cases that were far beyond my expertise. In those days, the IRS had a program called TCMP, taxpayer compliance measure program, which was essentially a program that required investigations on big tax cases to start right away.

I got lucky. I was hanging out at the office when a big case involving the second-largest brokerage firm in the world came into our squad. My father had just died the previous week, and I think to take my mind off things, my boss gave me the case to examine.

I was 25, and I was examining a giant of its industry. I remember arriving and not knowing how to find or get into the men's room. I felt very out of place. I started working on the case, and I remember noticing that the people who worked for the taxpayer-company were apprehensive since they saw that I was a sharp revenue agent. They knew I could do my job.

I did a great job on the case, and that is how I really got started. It gave me confidence that though I did not even know what a brokerage firm was when I started my investigation, I could learn.

I worked at that job for under four years. Most of the men working with me were also single, so we would go play baseball together on the weekends or nights I did not have school. We were very social, and everyone was supportive. It was a fun job because every day, it was a different job—I was investigating actors, businesspeople, regular people, you name it.

Everyone is afraid of revenue agents, so it was also a prestigious job, even though it did not pay well.

When I graduated law school in 1952, I was ripe; I was ready to tear up the world! I had worked for the Treasury Department, I had my law degree, and I was a certified public accountant. I was ready to be plucked. In 1953, I was assigned a case at a Wall Street law firm, which took a liking to me. After the case concluded, the law firm offered me at a good job at about a 70 percent pay increase, so I accepted.

My friends at the IRS made me a nice dinner, and I went off to success.

By this time, everyone knew two things about me. Number one: They knew I was good. And number two: They knew I was honest. There were some reprehensible people who did bad things, but I was straightforward and never wanted to know anything about impropriety. I told people directly that if I knew about illegal activity, I would have them arrested.

My reputation and integrity enabled me to enjoy a better type of work. When banks and big brokerage firms needed legitimate services, they would come to me. I brought in a lot of business, and in due time, I became a partner. Then I brought in even more business.

Eventually, the senior partners of the firm quit and started their own firm. They asked me to represent them, so I quit as well, and I started my own firm. The partners became my first clients with great success.

VICTOR POSNER

I built my practice differently than most others. Most lawyers go to State Bar meetings and hustle. I never hustle. I built my practice by representing people who thought I did a good job. All of my income comes from successful recommendations.

Many, many years ago, in the 1960s, when my practice was starting to build, I got a call from a client of mine, a stockbroker.

"A client of mine has a big tax case. His name is Victor Posner. Could you talk to him?"

I said, "Sure."

He handed the phone over, and Posner explained his case to me.

"How much money do you think I can win?" he asked after telling me the story.

"I cannot tell you that anymore than I can tell you what your watch is worth over the phone."

"Would you be interested in taking this case?"

"Sure."

Six months later, Posner called me up and said, "Remember me? I'm in town from Miami, and I would like to come to your office tomorrow morning."

"Tomorrow is Sunday," I said. "I will not be in the office."

"Then meet me in the penthouse of the Regency Hotel at 9 o'clock."

I did not know who Victor Posner was. My client said he was the largest owner of real estate in Miami, so at 9 o'clock, I knocked on the penthouse door of the Regency Hotel, holding a cigar in my other hand.

Have you ever put out your hand, and the other person refuses to shake it? Because that's what happened when Victor Posner opened the door.

"Put that God-damned cigar out," Posner said.

It was 9 o'clock in the morning on a Sunday in the freezing cold of winter, and Posner was wearing a pair of pajama pants. I was not in the mood for this.

"Please," I corrected him. "*Please* put that God-damned cigar out."

Posner looked me straight in the eye and said, "*Please* put that God-damned cigar out."

He pointed to a desk piled with papers.

"Look them over and tell me what you think."

"I will take them to the office and get back to you," I said.

"No. If you want this case, look at them here, or don't look at them at all."

He had paid a $500,000 deficiency to the IRS, and he was suing to get it back. That's how smart folks handle it: They pay the deficiency, and then they sue to get it back. If they win, they collect interest. Only deadbeats fail to pay IRS bills. Smart people pay them, even if they think they can get them back.

I took a look at the papers.

After a few minutes, I said, "Throw it out the window. You are not getting that money back."

"My accountant says I will get it back."

"I couldn't care less what your accountant says. You are not getting that money back."

Posner picked up the phone and called his accountant, a guy named Henry.

"I'm standing here with a young man from the bank who says I'm not getting that $500,000 payment back," he said. (He didn't want to tell his accountant that he was looking for a tax lawyer.)

"You're getting your money back," said Henry.

"Well, this young man from the bank thinks you are nuts."

"Tell him that he is nuts," said Henry. Then he added, "I will look into it. Let me call you back."

Two hours later, Henry still had not called him back. I was right, and he knew it.

Posner told me he was interviewing three other lawyers beside me and that he would get back to me. When I left the Regency Hotel, I walked past the former Commissioner of the Internal Revenue Service, who was on his way to the next interview with Posner. I really wanted Posner's business, but I figured there was no way I was getting it.

On Thursday, Posner called me, "Do you have any banks that would recommend you?"

I assured him that I did. He called me a couple of hours later and said, "The case is yours. Come back over."

So I went running back to his penthouse at the Regency. I was young and hungry.

"There is only one problem," he said. "I do not like to pay fees."

"That is a big problem. I have three kids."

"You will get a percentage of what you save me on this case," he clarified. "How much do you want?"

His terms were fine with me. I had a lot of confidence in my ability by that point. I was good, but I was also young and stupid, so I said, "Ten percent."

Victor Posner was then my client for life and generated substantial fees to my firm. He favored me to serve on many boards of directors of public companies, which he chaired, and was responsible for business from other clients.

SOL BERGER

M y wife's cousin, Richard Kurtz, married into a very wealthy family. His father-in-law was a man named Sol Berger, who was the president of Colonial Corporation of America, which was a major public company and the first public company to manufacture white dress shirts for men after World War II. Sol was a fun man.

When Richard first met his future father-in-law, Sol mentioned that the Colonial Corporation of America was having some tax problems. Richard, wanting to impress Sol, said, "Listen, my cousin Joan's husband, Marty, is a tax lawyer."

Sol responded with, "I do not want to meet any of your flunky relatives."

It wasn't very gracious, and long story short, Sol ended up feeling bad about that response. To appease Richard, he called me and asked me to come his office. Sol assumed that he would talk with me and see how stupid I was.

I drove into New Jersey for a meeting with Sol at the headquarters of Colonial Corporation of America. I was seated around a conference room table with Sol, as well as with his lawyers and accountants. I looked at the papers, and I noticed some technical issues.

I started asking questions. Did they look at this? Did they look at that?

"Of course we did!"

"But you came to the wrong result," I said.

"What does that mean?" Sol asked. "I just paid millions of dollars to get these results."

"And they were the wrong results," I assured him. He was beginning to wonder, looking at his cohorts, who did not know which end was up.

"What are you doing tomorrow?" he asked. It was Monday night.

"Whatever you want me to."

"Meet me in my New York office."

On Tuesday, I found more mistakes. Long story short, instead of washing me out, he hired me. I represented him for fifty years, recovering substantial dollars from the Internal Revenue Service.

I am still the trustee of Sol's estate.

MARTIN ROSEN & COMPANY, AND ROSEN & READE

When I resigned from my Wall Street firm, I started a law firm and an accounting firm. The accounting firm was just me, Martin Rosen & Company. For the law firm, I needed a partner, and therefore, I hired an old friend, Leonard Reade. We formed Rosen & Reade.

People hired me for both accounting work and tax law, which was very unusual in those days. The ruling against Bercu, the CPA who provided unlicensed legal work, was still fresh.

But I had licenses for both accounting and legal work. I had stationery for both. There was nothing anyone could do to me, even though they would have liked to. And in due time, the hybrid model of merging an accounting firm with a tax law firm became accepted, and even desired. I was fortunate to be at the forefront of this.

I became successful quickly, and I started hiring one man, two men, some women. I had no trouble finding clients. At that time, most accountants and attorneys who reached success did it by joining big firms and advancing through the firm to partner. I joined a big firm, and then I quit and created my own. At the top of my business, I had more than 100 people working in both firms.

Lawyers and accountants get their business, usually, from going to Bar Association meetings and joining organizations. I did some of that, but I did not get my business that way. I got my business from one source: satisfied customers. If Joe Client had a problem, and he came to me, I would provide excellent service. His buddy would then have a problem, and Joe would say, "I have the guy for you. Don't go anywhere else."

I knew every item in my office. I saw every bill that went out. I saw every document that was sent out. For a while, I saw every letter that was sent out. I worked 24/7, but I was a tough guy for excellence because I figured excellence would get me more business.

And it did.

Business became extraordinary.

But at the time, my accountant friends were afraid to send clients to my law firm because they knew I could take the client's accounting matters as well. And vice versa.

I decided to run both companies separately so that I would have no legal improprieties. My lawyers were only lawyers; my accountants were only accountants.

In the course of trying to build up an empire like this, I made mistakes with people. I was too easy. I let friendship get in the way, and it was stupid. Sometimes, if I hired somebody that I knew was not good, I turned my cheek.

One of my partners was a very good-looking man, but in due time, I came to realize that he was too busy looking in the mirror at his good-looking face and his good-looking wife to do his job. His clients started asking me to give them second opinions on many of his matters, and I realized that he was not doing his job in a satisfactory and competent manner.

I should have fired him then.

Instead, at the end of the year, I sat down with him, as I did with every employee, to give him his bonus and discuss his next year's compensation. I told him what his compensation would be, which I thought was very generous. It was too much.

I had recently invited him, his good-looking wife, and several of the other partners to my house for dinner. During that end-of-year meeting, I came to realize that he and his wife were unhappy that my house was much nicer than his.

He told me as much, and he said the compensation package I was offering was not sufficient. Fortunately, my wife is a very smart woman, and she taught me to ask questions during confrontations. I can be a bulldog, but Joan says to sit back and listen.

I remembered her advice, and I asked him this: "How much do you think you should make?"

He told me, so I asked: "How much do you think I should make?"

"About $100,000 more than me."

"Okay," I said. "Have you brought in any business this year?"

"No."

"Did you read the tax code this year?" I asked.

"No."

"Are you responsible for all of the legal and human resource obligations of this firm?"

"No."

"Let us talk about this. I bring in 100 percent of the business. I arrive earlier than you, and I leave later than you. I'm more educated than you. I know much more than you. I keep everyone here employed. I am the one responsible for all the obligations and legal requirements of running a company. And I should make only $100,000 more than you?"

And then I said, "I am going to fire you."

I fired him and gave him a year's severance, which he was not entitled to.

He never spoke to me again.

The lesson is that you really need to be a bit of a hard person if you want to be fair, and that is a terrible burden. At the end of the year, I had to take 40 or 50 people and decide what I thought was fair. If business was good, I wanted them to be happy. If I made a little less so they made a little more, I did not really care.

These are the things that take time and attention, and I made some mistakes until the very end. I had two partners who, while I was in the hospital, colluded to leave my firm and take business with them. It was not that they were leaving; people have a right to go out on their own. In fact, I want my employees and partners to succeed. But I want them to do it ethically. They went behind my back at a time when I needed to be looked after by the people I had always looked out for.

When I returned, they said to me, "We are putting in our notice."

I said, "I have a better idea. Leave now."

Do not get me wrong, I hired some terrific employees, and I elevated them. I succeeded in being economically successful, but I made mistakes because it was impossible to ascertain everything. I was trying to do too much in a job that I could not do. I was doing everything. I was playing golf, I was raising money for charity, I was traveling.

I needed honest administrative and personnel employees who could report to me and tell me who, in turn, was honest. I would give my right arm to get out of being an administrator and telling people when to go to work. I don't want to do that anymore.

So, in due time, I hired some administrators, and they have done a great job, and they are still my friends. But it came together because I cared, and I was competent. You have to have both—competence and caring—and then you have to hire people who are honest.

I did not always do that. I hired one of my buddies to help me run the accounting firm, and he decided to merge with two owners of another firm. After we merged, I found out that they had not paid their payroll in eight weeks. The owners said, "We told you that."

I said, "You sure as hell didn't. If you had told me that, I would have run for the door."

Accounting was not my true love; I loved the law. When I decided that I was done with accounting, I packed up and sold my accounting company.

SONNENSCHEIN, NATH & ROSENTHAL

By 2001, Rosen & Reade was a prestigious boutique law firm, and I got a call from Sonnenschein Nath & Rosenthal. At the time, Sonnenschein was in the top 75 largest law firms in the country, and it wanted to merge with Rosen & Reade because of my experience in trust, tax, and estates.

I said, "No way in hell."

After being convinced by some of the smarter people I had hired at Rosen & Reade, I saw that it was a good move. I could focus on what I liked doing best, and I would not have to manage any of the administrative aspects I had come to hate.

Just before the merger, Sonnenschein Nath & Rosenthal pulled the rug out from under my chair. They said they would take me and my top partner, a wonderful lawyer named Ralph Engel, but no one else.

I said, "Absolutely not. We all come, or none of us come."

And that is how Rosen & Reade merged with Sonnenschein Nath &

Rosenthal, which went on to become SNR Denton, the 29th largest law firm in the world, and then just Dentons, which today is the fourth largest law firm in the world by revenue. I worked at Dentons for the last two decades of my career, and I loved every minute of it.

RETIREMENT

I would say now that I made mistakes, but I made fewer mistakes than I hit home runs. I would like to memorialize my career as a big mosaic. I had clients who adored me, who knew they always got good results and a fair fee, and who knew that I went to battle for them. In a room with six or seven other people, I was on my clients' side, and I was running that meeting. I got most of the juice and the color out of the mosaic.

I said I would only retire if one of three things happened: One, they would carry me out, which they did not do. Two, I was not having a good time, which did not happen. Or number three, I felt that I was mentally compromised. I have too much ego to be a *schmuck*.

None of those three things happened. But it came time to retire when I was ninety-five, and I guess my timing was very good. I retired two weeks before the coronavirus pandemic lockdowns began.

Marty always said he was going to retire when he stopped being on top of his game. That never really happened.

—Avi Piontnica, partner at Dentons

Dad has always been a role model to everyone around him. He was so ethical that the same clients stayed with him for life. He worked well into his 90s, which kept him young, active, and always sharp-minded.

—Ted Karkus, my son-in-law

My colleagues planned an elaborate retirement party for me, but of course that could not happen because of the pandemic-related shutdowns. Instead, on September 15, 2020, they held a virtual retirement party for me.

Never being much for technology, and with the help of my sons-in-law, I managed to make my way onto a computer for a Zoom farewell. Following are some edited versions of the toasts that were delivered on that day.

RALPH ENGEL

Retired Partner, Dentons US New York Trusts,
Estates and Wealth Preservation Group

———————————

I t was the summer of 1990, and I got a call from a headhunter asking me if I had an interest in leaving the firm I was at. I was not interested and told her as much.

Then the headhunter said, "The firm is Rosen & Reade, where Marty Rosen is."

I knew of Marty, a well-known, very well-respected, brilliant, entrepreneurial trusts and estates, corporate, and tax lawyer. In the fall of 1990, Marty and I met for the first time. Although it took some time, it did not take too much for Marty to convince me to leave where I had been for fifteen years and come join him.

I joined Rosen & Reade in March of 1991, and I have had the pleasure of having Marty not only as my partner, but more importantly, as my friend all these years. It was one of the smartest moves I ever made.

Now fast forward to early 2001. Ten years had passed since I joined Marty. In early 2001, the same headhunter called me again, this time on behalf *of a firm that I had never heard of called Sonnenschein Nath & Rosenthal, the original predecessor in the United States of what is now Dentons US.*

Sonnenschein's plan was to absorb Rosen & Reade into Sonnenschein to create a trusts and estates department for New York.

I had to convince Marty to speak to the people involved. We met repeatedly with various Sonnenschein partners in New York and in Chicago. The proposal was to absorb all of Rosen & Reade into some Sonnenschein—but then the proposal changed. Suddenly, a proposal was given to Marty and me, letting us know that we would get paid more money if just the two of us joined Sonnenschein.

But Marty, who is the world's most loyal person, said, "Absolutely not. Turn that down. We are all coming together. There is no way I will abandon the rest."

On July 1, 2001, we joined what was then Sonnenschein and is now Dentons US. Most of us from Rosen & Reade remained at Dentons the rest of our careers, and some are still there. We are all lucky to have Marty by our side.

Marty has a magnetic personality. People instantly like him. He has a brilliant mind and is a remarkable problem solver. But most of all, Marty is a true friend and always has been. I would do most anything for Marty, and he would do the same for me.

MARGARET DEMARINO

Senior Trust & Estate Administrator at Dentons US LLP

In 1990, I worked for a large law firm in New York City. The law firm had many offices across the country, and our location had many floors in a luxurious building on Park Avenue. It was my first job out of college, and I was not looking to make a move.

One day I received a call from a recruiter saying that she had a fabulous job opportunity for me. To be quite honest, I had no interest, but I figured that I could always use the interview experience.

A few days later, I headed to Rosen & Reade at 757 Third Avenue. I met with one of the senior Trusts and Estates attorneys there, Donald Spanton, who interviewed me and then asked if I had any questions.

In those days, we did not have Google, so I couldn't do a lot of research about the firm before the interview. The recruiter had not given me much information, so I started by asking, "How many offices do you have across the country?"

He replied, "One. This is it."

I then asked, "How many floors do you have in the building?"

He replied, "One. This is it, and we share the floor with our sister accounting firm, Martin Rosen & Company."

I then asked, "I have an office where I'm working now. Will I have an office here?"

Mr. Spanton replied, "No. You are going to be in a room that is divided into four. You will be sharing it with three other paralegals."

At that moment, I was thinking, "Alright, this interview is pretty much over. Maybe if I hurry, I can get lunch before I head back to the office."

Mr. Spanton said, "On the way out, let's see if we can stop by and say a quick hello to Marty Rosen. He's the head of our firm."

Wanting to be polite, I agreed to say hello to this Mr. Rosen, even though I knew that meant I would need to forego lunch before going back to my office.

When we got to Mr. Rosen's office, I remember him waving me in and saying, "Take a seat. I will be right with you."

My first impression of Mr. Rosen was that he was the best multitasker I had ever seen. He was dictating while he was on the phone with a client, and he was writing something down, and talking to his secretary.

I sat there in awe, thinking, "I just do not know how this man does this."

He finished with what he was doing, and then he sat and talked to me for a while. I remember thinking, "There's something so special about this man." He made me feel so at ease right off the bat.

And that's Mr. Rosen's true talent. No matter how busy he is, he always makes you feel like the most important person.

I thought to myself, "If I have the opportunity to work with this man, I have to take it." I figured, "He is 65, so if I get to work with him for the next five years or so, I'll get some good experience before he retires."

It was the best decision I ever made. We would work together for the next thirty years. Mr. Rosen would often joke that he would retire when I retire.

If people asked me to describe Mr. Rosen, there are so many words I could choose. Intelligent: absolutely. He has a photographic memory. His knowledge about the law and accounting is incomparable. He is versatile: He worked for the IRS as a treasury agent. He was the mayor of Lawrence. He was the founder of two successful firms: Rosen & Reade and Martin Rosen & Company. He is charismatic, which goes without saying.

But if I had to use only one word, it would be this: loyal. Mr. Rosen is loyal to his clients. I think that every single one of them has his cell phone number, and they call him 24/7. And even though he is retired now, he will never say, "Please stop bothering me. I'm retired."

He takes all those calls.

And he is loyal to everyone who has ever worked for him. We all know that no matter what, Mr. Rosen always had our back.

There is a saying that loyalty begets loyalty. And that is so true of Mr. Rosen. And it is also why he is just so beloved by all of us.

Mr. Rosen has been my mentor for 30 years. The knowledge that I have gained during that time is invaluable. But besides that knowledge, he has taught me so many valuable life lessons. He played a big part in the person and professional I have become, and I am so grateful to him.

ELLIOTT PORTNOY

CEO of Dentons

Marty is one of the reasons our firm is stronger, better, and kinder than when we started. Mark Twain said age is an issue of mind over matter; if you don't mind, it doesn't matter. As long as I have known Marty, age frankly has never mattered at all—never been a relevant part of the discussion.

In 2015 or 2016, Martin told me that he would be practicing for another twenty or thirty years. Age never mattered.

But what always mattered to him is his family, his clients, his community, and his team. These are the guideposts he set for himself, and for us all.

The leaders of the firm learned from the examples Marty set.

I have had the pleasure of talking to Marty about many topics over a long period of time. It was always talk because Marty was not a big fan of email. With every conversation we ever had, no matter what the topic was at the beginning—his kids, his grandkids, his great grandkids, and his family—the conversation always ended with a conversation about how my family was doing, because *he cared deeply about that.*

And it did not matter what the topic was, no matter how tough the conversation might have been. He never focused on taking credit or scoring points. He only wanted to talk about how he could make people's lives better.

It was no different when I saw him in the hallways. Most of us walked; Marty jogged. He would be at one end of the hall and exuberantly bound down the hall to give me a hug or a handshake, or maybe both. We would talk about a big new case he landed, something the family had done, perhaps one of the grandchildren got into college, and how we could do even better together as a firm.

It is because of him that our reputation exists as one of the premier practices to advise high-net-worth individuals and families: his tireless efforts, his sophistication, his integrity, his commitment to excellence. He was a friend and a legend who taught us all about what matters most in practice and, more importantly, in life.

MIKE MCNAMARA

Partner and Former CEO, Dentons US

I n April of 2020, due to the coronavirus pandemic, we had to suspend an entire committee that was planning a retirement party for Marty. We wanted to have the party in person and worthy of his power of goodness.

Even though he never liked email much, and even though he retired, Marty kept coming through with pieces of advice during the pandemic. He was ever-present.

I remember one of the most recent times we were together. Marty and I were having one of his hallway conversations about how my family was doing and how the firm was doing. Marty briefed me on the team. It was always about the team—not about him or his accomplishments, but about the team. He shared with me that he had never been busier.

"People, people are needing us all over the place," he said.

It was great to see that level of enthusiasm ever present in everything he did. And it was beyond just our team. What he inspired in the next *generation was the passion of his avocations and the work that he did for the Simon Wiesenthal Center. He enlightened and shared with us that which goes to the heart of our humanity, the heart of our vision, the heart of who we are as a firm. It was more than just the work. It was more than just the people. It was always about where we could go together, learning from the past, but always living in the moment and building for the future.*

Ralph Engel, me, and Ralph Kelley at the
2003 Sonnenschein Nath & Rosenthal Christmas Party.

RALPH KELLEY

Retired Senior Counsel of Dentons

Marty and I were together for twenty-five years. I have many fond memories, all of them good, but two instances stand out. The first was when Marty and I represented one of his clients in an IRS audit. I remember sitting across the table from four revenue agents. On our side of the table, there were just the two of us. Our combined age at that time was 170 years. And our combined years of practice at that time, was 110. So I think we set some kind of record.

The second instance that really stands out in my memory was from 2010 when he and Joan were vacationing in Europe. Someone told him that my wife, Betty, had died.

Marty and Joan cut their vacation short. They came back early, just to be at Betty's funeral. That was a magnificent act of kindness and friendship.

NANCY FERRARA

Executive Assistant

NANCY: Hi Mr. Rosen.

MARTY: Hi Nancy, I miss you how you doing?

NANCY: This is very hard. It has been a privilege to work for you. It was over twenty years ago that you made me an offer I couldn't refuse. I remember it clearly. It was one of the best decisions of my life.

MARTY: Sometimes you regretted it, right? Sometimes you regretted it.

NANCY: No, I haven't regretted it.

The first few months working for you, I remember, that I had to learn how to approach you with certain phone calls. I remember receiving a couple of phone calls and interrupting you in meetings or business dinners and being unsure about interrupting you.

But your response to these interruptions was, "You have a real eye for business, and thank you for the interruptions." They were well appreciated.

Unfortunately, I did have to call you out of many meetings about clients that had passed away, but I always knew that you wanted to know immediately.

Through the years, you met my family and my nephew, who is now 27. I don't know if you remember this, but when my nephew came to see you, he was still in high school. You said one sentence to him, and that sentence was, "There are no shortcuts in life." He did not want to go to college, but he did end up going to college after hearing that, and he graduated.

It has been my honor to work for you.

Nancy Ferrara, me, and Margaret DeMarino.

ILENE ROSEN COHEN

Former Employee

My dad is fiercely loyal to the people he cares about, and he is extremely charitable—and not just in the monetary sense. He is generous in giving his time, and he has always taught us to do the same.

One day, I said to him, "Daddy, show me how to pay the bills. God forbid something happens to you, I want to know what I need to pay." And he had a stack of bills that reached the ceiling. These were for him to donate to what seemed like a thousand charities.

Yes, there are major charities in which he is involved in, but he will never not give to charities for veterans or disabled people. He would never say no when it came to helping someone.

He is also generous with his employees and clients.

I'm an attorney, and I worked for my dad for five years, so I got to see the professional side of him. He had a very successful firm, and he advised his clients in the most personal way. They were not his friends, but they became his friends. He took their problems to heart, as if they were his own. And he was proud of their successes.

He is retired, but he still speaks with his clients all of the time. Whenever I go to his house, he is sitting at his desk, doing paperwork, and always on the phone. He keeps in contact with everybody from all stages of his life.

As a boss, he was demanding. He was exacting and not easy. It was his way or the highway because he is a perfectionist. But he was fiercely loyal to the people he respected. He still takes care of his secretary and his right hand, even though he is retired.

He said to me, "Make sure that you continue these gifts once I am gone."

The partners at Rosen & Reade, pictured left to right: Philip Michaels, Ralph Kelley, Lewis Schwartz, Ralph Engel, Lawrence Blatte, Martin Rosen, Erwin Hass, Richard Carter, Kevin Groarke, and Michael Shlesinger.

PART FOUR

Joan and me in 1954.

JOAN

While I was in law school, I looked at marriage as a burden. I had a six-person study group. The five of us who were single did well, but the sixth guy dropped out. He could not manage the workload because he had responsibilities at home. I wanted to establish my career and reach some level of success before I added the responsibilities of marriage.

I was making good money—I made $25,000 in the second year the Wall Street firm, and I thought I was a zillionaire. I was living with my mother, who was recently widowed, and my brother. I was making enough money to financially care for my mother while Leon was her caregiver. It was a different generation, and no one counted their money. I was taking care of my brother and my mother, and they were taking care of me.

I was not even thinking about marriage. Being single helped me bring in more business. I was a bachelor with no obligations. I had no place to be except law school, and then, after graduating, my job.

When I was twenty-eight, I had quit the IRS and graduated law school, so that summer was the first summer I could enjoy my life. All of my buddies and I would travel to the Borscht Belt in the Catskills to play baseball. (*Borscht* is a Yiddish word that means soup.) All the old Jewish actors and comedians would visit the Borscht Belt as well, so in September of 1953, the United Jewish Appeal sponsored a weekend for single Jewish men and women in the area.

My buddies and I were all a little older—most of us were in our late twenties, including me. My rule was that I did not date young Jewish women because after the second date, their fathers wanted us to get married. Instead, I dated Jewish women my age, whose fathers were not quite as imposing.

I will never forget. I was checking into the hotel the first day, and as I walked to the front desk to check in, I saw a lovely girl wearing a red dress. I walked over to her, and I introduced myself. She was absolutely gorgeous.

"Little lady in red, would you have champagne with me?"

Her answer was a very good one. She said, "Only if you invite my friends," which I did.

Her name was Joan. She was an only child, the daughter of a dentist, and she lived in an affluent suburban area called Belle Harbor near the Atlantic Ocean. I spent a little bit of time talking to her. When I learned she was only nineteen, though, I decided not to bother with her too much that weekend. Men my age were looking for different things, and the young Jewish women were being proper.

On Sunday, when we checked out, the men took many telephone numbers. She was the cutest person there by far, so I took her number.

I did not call, though, because the next week, my firm sent me to California. I was still working at the Wall Street firm, which wanted to start an office in California. Since I was a bachelor, it made sense that I would go on the trip, and perhaps even transfer to California, a choice I eventually decided against because I wanted to be with my mother to help take care of her after my father's death.

I spent some time in California, and when I came back, I had Joan's number in my wallet. Joan had the good sense to make sure I invited her friends to have drinks with us when we first met, and a buddy who had gone on the trip with me was dating one of Joan's friends.

He said, "You're a schmuck. She's a nice girl, and very pretty. Give her a chance."

Keep in mind that it had been eight weeks since I asked for her number, so when I called her up for a date, she was not too happy.

"I am busy," she said. Period. She didn't ask if I was available another night. She just said, "I am busy."

I just thought, *Okay, sister. That's it.*

Fortunately, my buddy's girlfriend said to Joan, "You are making a mistake. Give him a chance."

Joan and me on our wedding day.

My brother, Leon; my mother, Kate; me; the beautiful bride; my father-in-law, Al George
Rosenblum; and my mother-in-law, Beatrice (Kurtz) Rosenblum.

We started dating in 1953. Her parents were nice people. She was their only child, so she was their whole world. She lived far from me, and I never wanted her to take a car, so I always picked her up. She lived about an hour away from me, and it was a pain in the neck, but it was worth it. About eight months later, we were engaged, and we married on February 6, 1955.

We have been married for sixty-eight years. She is a great woman, a great mother, and a great wife.

I paid my dues, but I got lucky. I got all good things back

When he first called me, I wasn't so nice. I was very abrupt. I was a lot angry because I had really wanted him to call me, and then he didn't for eight weeks.

Then a friend said to me that I was making a mistake. She was dating one of his friends, so she knew Marty a bit. She said he was a nice man, and she encouraged me to call him, so I did.

We went to a neighborhood meeting place called Anthony's for our first date. After about six months of dating, I knew I wanted it to be him.

First of all, he was very handsome. That sounds superficial, but the truth is that he was good to look at. He was charming. From a practical standpoint, he was successful. He was attentive, and he was a leader. I never considered myself to be a leader, so I admired that quality in him. Everyone looked up to him and revered him. He was everyone's favorite.

He was all the things you would want in a husband, and I fell in love with him. He wasn't a wise guy. He had a naivety about him that made him very sincere and transparent, and I felt very lucky. It was obvious to me that he was a good and likable person."

—**Joan**

Joan and me in the 1960s.

I always tell my girls how lucky they are that I was so smart because he picked me, and I picked him. I always think they should be grateful that I was so young to know a quality person when I saw him. I knew immediately that he was very special. And I feel blessed that he loves me, and I love him. We have had sixty-eight marvelous years together, mostly all upward, and wonderful.

—Joan

Joan and me in our sixties.

Joan and me on our sixtieth wedding anniversary. Joan is still, by far, the cutest person in the room.

The other day, my dad said, "Why don't you take your mom shopping. She's been wearing a lot of black lately."

He loves color, and I think it's cute that he notices. Sometimes he will look at her and say, "You look good today." It's cute. Most days you will find them matching in color. They claim it is always by accident and a factor of being married for over sixty years.

—Nancy Rosen Stern, our youngest daughter

My dad is very close with my mom. He runs everything by her. They are a partnership. He values her opinion a lot.

Behind the scenes, there is no decision they make without her approval. He always looked to her for advice and for guidance. He would come home and tell his stories about the day, and she would give her opinion.

—Ilene Rosen Cohen, my oldest daughter

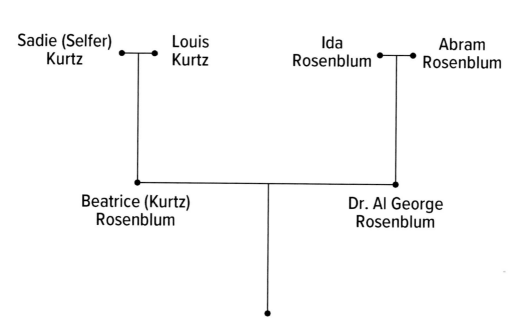

Sadie (Selfer) Kurtz   Louis Kurtz   Ida Rosenblum   Abram Rosenblum

Beatrice (Kurtz) Rosenblum   Dr. Al George Rosenblum

Joan (Rosenblum) Rosen
born January 5, 1934

MARRIED LIFE

Jewish husbands in New York live where their wives want to live. Joan wanted to be closer to her parents in Queens. I wanted to stay close to my mom in Westchester, so we decided to rent in Forest Hills, Queens. Forest Hills is a high-rise community filled with young people. Joan found a beautiful building on a beautiful street. The building had an elevator and as a circular driveway with a doorman. It cost $131 per month. I thought that was a ridiculous sum of money. I did not want to pay it; Joan did, so we took it.

No other young people were living there because no young people could afford $131 a month. Joan and I had two incomes, though. Joan was working as a schoolteacher, and I was working at my own firm.

One of my clients was an older man who lived nearby and would pick me up in his chauffeured limousine and drop me off at the office.

Each morning, the doorman would ring the bell and say, "Mr. Rosen, your father is here." He figured that if Joan and I were able to pay $131 as a young couple, I must have a rich father!

When I was growing up, my grandfather had a chauffeur and a limo. He would often drive the grandkids to school. My sister and brother would request to be dropped two blocks away. I was so proud to be with my grandfather, that I would tell him, "Drop me off right up front."

—Bari Klein Cohen, my granddaughter

On May 17, 1957, our first daughter, Ilene, was born. We had lived in the apartment for four years, and we wanted more kids, so it was time to move. Joan and I bought a house in Lawrence, a primarily Jewish suburban community in Nassau County, which is on Long Island. We were surrounded by young people, and it was a good life.

I had wanted a son, and back in those days, there was no way to tell whether a woman was pregnant with a boy or a girl. When Joan was in labor with Ilene, I waited in the hospital lobby with a baseball bat to give to my future son, only to meet Ilene instead. By 1960, Joan was pregnant again, so I took that same baseball bat to the hospital and waited with it.

Lynn was born on March 23, 1960.

On June 9, 1965, I went to the hospital again with that baseball bat, eagerly awaiting the birth of my third child, which I assumed would be a boy. The odds were in our favor.

I remember the doctor coming out and saying, "I don't know what your other two girls look like, but this one is beautiful."

Me with my daughters in Washington, D.C. in 1974. Pictured left to right: Ilene, Nancy, me, Lynn.

He has never once complained or been disappointed that he did not have a son. We have a beautiful family together, and no one has ever given us a minute of problems or tears. They are wonderful children, and I am a lucky girl.

—Joan

Pictured left to right: Nancy, Lynn, Joan, me, and Ilene.

Every time my dad went to the hospital when my mom was giving birth, he took a baseball bat and sat in the hospital lobby, waiting to take a picture of their son with a baseball bat.

But he had three daughters.

And now, he wouldn't change a thing, not for the world. The way he learned to make a relationship with each of these girls and women in his life—it's amazing.

—Ilene Rosen Cohen, our oldest daughter

OUR DAUGHTERS

Ilene, Lynn, and Nancy are off the charts. They call me all the time—every day. They could not be nicer. They all live within a mile of us, in a nice little neighborhood.

Top row: Ilene, Lynn, and Nancy. Bottom row: Me and Joan.

I give credit to my wife for my family. She did it all, not me. I was there, but I wasn't there. The best example I could give you is from Nancy's birthday party.

I traveled quite a lot, and I rarely was at their school events or birthday parties. And I remember once calling my wife from an airport on a Friday afternoon to let her know I would not be home.

"You have to be home."

"I cannot," I said.

Joan was not happy, and she told me at a minimum to call back later so that I could wish Nancy a happy birthday. When I called Nancy, she called all her friends to the phone so that they could listen in.

"My father is on the phone! It's my dad!" she was saying. She was our third child, and so many of her friends had parents who were divorced. Her friends never saw me, so they didn't believe Nancy had a dad.

I felt bad that I had to be introduced by proxy. I'm not saying I was the worst father in the world, but I was not the greatest. Joan was there, though, for everything. Thank God she was there because the kids were good kids. They earned good grades, they did not do drugs, and they really never got into trouble. That was all Joan. She did a great job, and I got lucky with that.

You can tell that they love us back by the fact that they all live within a mile radius of us! They have good attitudes. We got lucky, but most of it was because of Joan.

Lynn, Nancy, and Ilene with me at
Nancy and Steven's wedding on May 29, 1988.

Those years were a little bit tough, but I understood.
Marty was not out on the town; he was working.
He was achieving for his family, and he took great
care to share everything with me. I felt that I was part
of the team, and I was always proud to be
sitting next to him.

—Joan

A family picture taken at Temple Beth Shalom on February 25, 1968, in Lawrence, NY. I was being honored by the United Jewish Association. Bottom row: Lynn and Ilene. Top row: Joan, me, and Nancy.

Lynn, Ilene, Joan, Nancy, and me, in late December of 1977, or early January of 1978.

ILENE

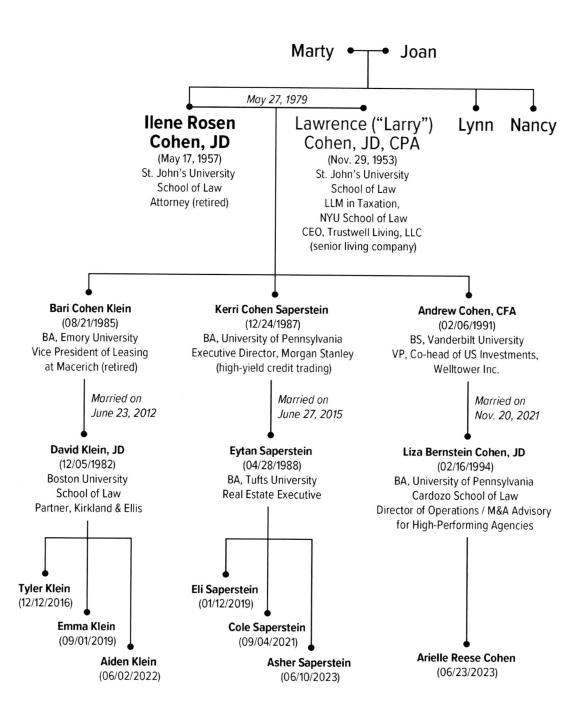

Marty ●━━━● Joan

May 27, 1979

Ilene Rosen Cohen, JD
(May 17, 1957)
St. John's University
School of Law
Attorney (retired)

Lawrence ("Larry") Cohen, JD, CPA
(Nov. 29, 1953)
St. John's University
School of Law
LLM in Taxation,
NYU School of Law
CEO, Trustwell Living, LLC
(senior living company)

Lynn   **Nancy**

Bari Cohen Klein
(08/21/1985)
BA, Emory University
Vice President of Leasing
at Macerich (retired)

*Married on
June 23, 2012*

Kerri Cohen Saperstein
(12/24/1987)
BA, University of Pennsylvania
Executive Director, Morgan Stanley
(high-yield credit trading)

*Married on
June 27, 2015*

Andrew Cohen, CFA
(02/06/1991)
BS, Vanderbilt University
VP, Co-head of US Investments,
Welltower Inc.

*Married on
Nov. 20, 2021*

David Klein, JD
(12/05/1982)
Boston University
School of Law
Partner, Kirkland & Ellis

Eytan Saperstein
(04/28/1988)
BA, Tufts University
Real Estate Executive

Liza Bernstein Cohen, JD
(02/16/1994)
BA, University of Pennsylvania
Cardozo School of Law
Director of Operations / M&A Advisory
for High-Performing Agencies

Tyler Klein
(12/12/2016)

Emma Klein
(09/01/2019)

Aiden Klein
(06/02/2022)

Eli Saperstein
(01/12/2019)

Cole Saperstein
(09/04/2021)

Asher Saperstein
(06/10/2023)

Arielle Reese Cohen
(06/23/2023)

My father gets very annoyed with bickering. He has no patience for it. He says, "This is family. Let it go. Let it go. Family first. Let it go." So everybody looks out for one another. We are very lucky. I don't know if my children will be this physically close, but they learned from my dad how to be close to each other.

—Ilene Rosen Cohen

Pictured left to right: Me, Joan, Larry and Ilene Cohen, Eytan and Kerri Saperstein, Bari and David Klein, and Liza and Andrew Cohen.

Pictured left to right: Larry, Ilene, Joan, and me. We are lucky because all three of our daughters married men who are like sons to us.

I lost my father when I was 44, and I don't want to take away from my relationship with him because he was wonderful. But if you had to pick someone to be your father-in-law, you cannot find a better person than Marty Rosen.

I am very lucky. I have great kids and great grandkids, and it starts with Marty. He is just incredible.

—Larry Cohen

Nancy, Lynn, Joan, me, Ilene, and Larry.

I am proud to say that my children and their families are continuing to advocate for Jewish causes. Here I am presenting Larry and Ilene with the Community Leadership award at the UJA Southshore of Long Island inaugural dinner. Joan and I received this same award years earlier.

Dad has been a role model and mentor to all his children and grandchildren. When I met Ilene, I had just graduated from college and was working in public accounting. I was exposed to various aspects of accounting and developed a keen interest in taxation. I sought Dad's advice and decided to attend law school and become a tax lawyer. When I graduated law school, I once again sought Dad's advice and accepted a position as an associate in Rogers & Wells tax department. I continued my legal education at night and received an LL.M in taxation. While in law school I also completed the Certified Public Accountant exam and now had the same degrees and designations as Dad. While I ultimately left the practice of law to enter the business world, I always felt that having the same education and background created a special bond between us. His interest and advice were invaluable in setting my career path.

—Larry Cohen

Top: Me with great-grandson Eli Saperstein.

Bottom: Me with great-grandson Aiden Klein.

Top: Me with my great-grandkids Tyler and Emma Klein. Bottom: Me with my great-grandson Cole Saperstein.

My dad has a very special relationship with each and every grandchild. He speaks to all of them weekly. My sister's son is a Division-I basketball player, and he follows every game.

My son was the first grandson, and the first boy in the family. He was the quarterback in high school, and he was injured his senior year. After he healed, his first game back was the championship game in the middle of winter during a torrential downpour. My dad and even my mom, who hates football, flew in, and they sat there in the stadium. They won the game. It was a great day for my son, and it was a great day for my dad.

I have a grandson who is six years old, who is very into sports, and my dad will call him on Sundays and say, "What do you think? Who is going to win the game?"

—Ilene Rosen Cohen

Left: My perfect newborn great-granddaughter Arielle Reese Cohen.

Right: Me with my perfect newborn great-grandson Asher Saperstein.

Bottom: Tyler Klein, Joan, me, and Eli Saperstein.

Papa Marty calls me before the games to ask me who is going to win. I look at the stats and guess, and then he places a bet.

Last year, in the World Series, I was going to tell him to choose the Astros, but it was too late. He bet on the Phillies, and the Astros won!

—Tyler Klein, my six-year-old bookie

Me with my great-grandson Tyler Klein.

Marty instills confidence in people and brings out the very best in them. When talking to his young grandkids or great grandkids, he refers to them as "Chairman of the Board" and other endearing terms that convey his love and respect for them. He talks about how special and incredible they are. He never places limits on the people in his family, instilling in them the belief that with hard work and dedication they can be anything they want. The result is that he elevates everyone around him.

—David Klein, my grandson-in-law

I speak to my grandparents on the phone as often as I speak to my parents.

—Bari Cohen Klein

Joan, our granddaughter Bari Cohen Klein, and me.

My granddaughter
Bari Cohen Klein and
me.

I am blessed to be a part of Marty's family. He is one of the most honorable people I know and should be extremely proud of all that he has accomplished. Marty has excelled in so many different aspects of life, but love for family is what really sets him apart. Marty has set the standard incredibly high for the rest of us, having lived a life of true purpose, guided by a set of principles based on justice and integrity, which we are passing down to our children. He has paved the way for all of us that follow, and we will do our best to make him proud.

—David Klein, my grandson-in-law

When I graduated college, I didn't know what I was going to do career-wise. Through my grandfather, I got an internship at Kenneth Cole. My grandfather always calls to check in, so he called me after my first day of work.

"How was work?"

I said, "It wasn't that good. The person I was supposed to report to is no longer at the company, so I don't have a job."

He was more upset than I was. "Give me five minutes." And sure enough, five minutes later, he called me back and said, "Tomorrow, you need to be at Newmark."

"What is Newmark?'"

"They're a real estate company."

"I don't know anything about real estate."

"That's okay. Most people who are in real estate don't know anything about real estate either. Be there in the morning. They are expecting you."

Turns out, he knew the head of Newmark, and within one phone call, I had a job the next day. I did well at Newmark, and when I graduated college, they offered me a full-time position, so I worked in commercial real estate for a year. After a while, as my grandfather would do, he called to check in. I told him that I didn't love it. I felt like I wasn't learning much.

At the time, we were planning a family trip to Los Angeles for an opening of Simon's office at the Museum of Tolerance, which was established by the Simon Wiesenthal Center. My grandpa asked me to stay in Los Angeles a few extra days.

"I want you to meet Mace Siegel," he said.

He explained that Mace was one of the founders of Macerich, which is the third-largest shopping development center in the world. Mace was also my grandfather's client. Mace was known as a godfather of Southern California horse racing, so we met at Santa Anita Park in California. And sure enough, Mace and I hit it off.

I went to work at Macerich, and when I retired after having my third child, I was vice president of leasing. My grandpa gave me the path to an amazing career.

He has done this with all of his kids and his grandkids, and so many other people. He is so well connected, and when someone asks him for a favor, he delivers in strides. He is always so gracious about it, too. He will say, "Luck is when opportunity meets preparation." He never takes credit.

He has instilled amazing values in not only me but our entire family. He has always been so charitable and generous. Because of him, David and I have become involved with many charitable causes."

—Bari Cohen Klein, our granddaughter

Me, our granddaughter-in-law Liza Bernstein Cohen, Joan, and our grandson Andrew.

From the moment I met Grandpa Marty, I knew he was special. To know him is to admire him. At 97 years of age, he can recall even the most insignificant details of his life experiences from a young age. His mind and memory are astonishing. The imprint he leaves on everyone he meets is a true testament to the man that he is and everything that he stands for. He has treated me as one of his own grandchildren and shares the same values of family, hard work, patriotism, and dedication to the Jewish people that have been engrained in me by my own grandfather. I feel so fortunate to learn from him, as he is truly a remarkable man.

I will never forget one vacation I went on with the entire Rosen/Cohen family. Andrew and I were not yet engaged. It was imminent, although I did not know it. We were taking family photos, and when it came time for the photo of the entire group, the photographer asked that the non-family members step out, referring to the unmarried significant others. Grandpa Marty immediately called me back into the photo and said to the photographer, "This young lady is family."

—Liza Bernstein Cohen

My dad always looks tough and opinionated, but there is also a sensitive and emotional side to him. I was watching the video of the day my son Andrew was married, and I noticed that he teared up when he watched Larry and me walk Andrew down the aisle.

—Ilene Rosen Cohen

Four generations at my grandson Michael Stern's wedding: Larry Cohen, Andrew Cohen, and me with Tyler Klein, Emma Klein, and Eli Saperstein.

At the Washington Monument with my granddaughter Kerri Cohen Saperstein and her wonderful husband Eytan Saperstein.

They don't make men like Papa Marty anymore. He is the greatest man I know. When they speak of "The Greatest Generation," it makes sense to me because I have had the privilege of seeing it firsthand with Papa Marty. In a word, he is an "All-American." He sets the standard across the board—with his love of family, service to his country, success in business, building of life-long relationships with friends, and his countless charitable endeavors. Papa Marty is THE role model, the epitome of a man that I strive to become. I am filled with humility and gratitude that I have the honor to be a part of the incredible family that he has created. And for my three young boys to have Papa Marty in their lineage! How lucky are we? Sergeant Marty, we salute you: for making us all better people, for practicing what you preach, for showing us what a life well-lived actually looks like. We love you.

—Eytan Saperstein

I always knew he was a true patriot, loving America to the fullest. The two of us went to a Yankees game many years ago, just the two of us. I was probably twelve at the time. These were the days before iPhones, Apple Pay, or even the use of credit cards for small purchases.

As we were walking into Yankees Stadium in a full crowd of people, my grandfather noticed a homeless veteran with a sign, asking for some money. Of course, being the patriot that he is, Grandpa didn't hesitate. He reached into his pocket and donated some small bills to the veteran.

As we made our way into the stadium, Grandpa offered to buy me a program and box of Cracker Jacks. When he reached into his pocket, he noticed that after giving money to the veteran, someone had pushed their way between my grandpa and me, in a ploy to pick-pocket him.

There we stood, at Yankees stadium with not a penny to spend, and although I could tell Grandpa was annoyed and frustrated, he didn't let it ruin the day. He still had no regrets that he had given that veteran some spare change, and we still had the best time together.

—Kerri Cohen Saperstein

Kerri, me,
and Bari.

Growing up, we all lived within a mile of each other. Monday Night Dinner was always at my grandparent's house. My grandma would prepare dinner, and everybody would eat at their house on Monday nights. We would go straight to their house from Hebrew school and would wait for my grandfather to arrive from the office.

My grandfather is the patriarch of our family. He is the reason we all stick together. He and my grandmother have instilled unbelievable values of family generosity and love. His ability to show an interest and be such a loving person has instilled a close-knit family. It really all stems from him.

—Bari Cohen Klein

In fifth grade, my class was tasked with interviewing and presenting on a significant person in our life.

Without hesitation, I knew Grandpa was the right person to interview, as he had to have had the best life story of anyone out there.

When I asked to interview him, Grandpa was thrilled.

Despite his extremely busy work schedule and my somewhat busy student-athlete schedule, he prioritized the time. I bought a Dictaphone and interviewed the most incredible man. We sat together for hours, over multiple sessions, in his den, as he recalled his life.

At such a young age I felt so honored and proud to be his granddaughter. I knew then and I know today that he is a true legend.

—Kerri Cohen Saperstein

I was the quarterback during my senior year in high school, and our team was in the big playoff game. My grandparents flew home from Florida just to watch that game, which was in the pouring rain. He is the guy who would never miss that game. I don't know many grandfathers who would do that.

—Andrew Cohen

Pictured left to right: Bari, Kerri, me, and Andrew.

Joan and me with Lynn, Ted, Brett, and Jason Karkus.

I had my kids later in life. I had Jason in 1997, and I didn't have Brett until 2002. I wanted Jason to have a sibling. My feeling was that if Jason didn't have siblings, he should at least be near his cousins and his relatives, so we moved close to my parents. And now we all live in this cocoon of a neighborhood right around the corner from each other.

—Lynn Rosen Karkus

LYNN

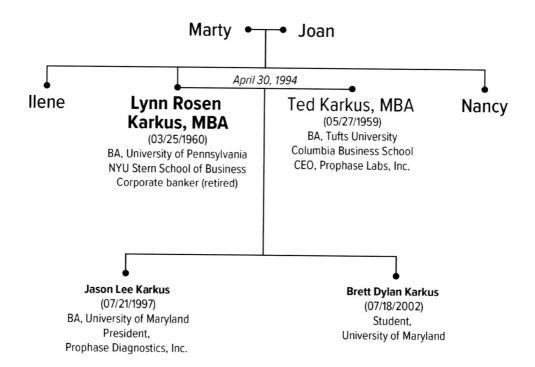

Marty ●──┬──● Joan

Ilene

April 30, 1994

Lynn Rosen Karkus, MBA
(03/25/1960)
BA, University of Pennsylvania
NYU Stern School of Business
Corporate banker (retired)

Ted Karkus, MBA
(05/27/1959)
BA, Tufts University
Columbia Business School
CEO, Prophase Labs, Inc.

Nancy

Jason Lee Karkus
(07/21/1997)
BA, University of Maryland
President,
Prophase Diagnostics, Inc.

Brett Dylan Karkus
(07/18/2002)
Student,
University of Maryland

One of the things I will always cherish about Grandpa is the reaction my brother and I get from him when we surprise him by stopping by the house to say hello.

—Jason Karkus

Joan and me with all eight of our beautiful grandchildren. Top row: Kerri Cohen Saperstein, me, and Bari Cohen Klein. Middle row: Andrew Cohen and Michael Stern. Front row: Samantha Stern, Joan, Brett Karkus, Corey Stern, and Jason Karkus.

Pictured left to right with all eight of my grandchildren and two of their spouses: David Klein, Andrew Cohen, Michael Stern, Samantha Stern, Corey Stern, Bari Klein, Joan, me, Kerri and Eytan Saperstein, Jason Karkus, and Brett Karkus.

What stands out about Dad has been his dedication to family and the standards that he continues to set for all of us to follow. It is not a coincidence that his three daughters have been happily married for many decades. I come from divorced parents, and yet Lynn and I have been married for close to thirty years, and still going strong. There is no question that Dad's example influenced me and us. These high standards of commitment to family are being passed on to his grandchildren, and even his great grandchildren.

—Ted Karkus

My father has an incredible ability to remember what each grandchild is doing every day. He calls them on the first day of school, the first day of work, the first day of practice, the first day of whatever. I always thought that was really remarkable because there are eight of them, and he is incredibly busy.

—Lynn Rosen Karkus

The family at Brett's Bar Mitzvah. Pictured left to right, top row: Corey, Steven, and Nancy Stern; Jason Karkus; me and Joan; Brett, Lynn and Ted Karkus; Larry and Andrew Cohen; Eytan Saperstein. Bottom row: Michael and Samantha Stern; Kerri Saperstein; Ilene Cohen; Bari and David Klein.

Pictured left to right in 2019: Jason, Brett, Lynn, and Ted Karkus; Michael, Corey, Samantha, Steven, and Nancy Stern; me and Joan; Ilene and Larry Cohen; Kerri, Eytan, and Eli Saperstein; Bari, Emma, Tyler, and David Klein; Andrew and Liza Cohen.

When I was young, everyone called me Little Marty. I remember being very upset because I didn't want to look like a man.

—Lynn Rosen Karkus

Joan and me with our three daughters: Nancy, Lynn, and Ilene.

My father had no sons, and he loves football. When I was young, he had season tickets to the Jets. My mother hated football, and she hated the cold, so I would go with him. I did not like football or understand it, but I wanted to spend the time with my dad.

My middle sister, Lynn, really loves sports, so when she got older, she went with him to the games. She went to spend time with him, of course, but also because she loves football. I was glad I could back off.

—Ilene Rosen Cohen

When we were young, my dad worked all the time. He worked like crazy. That was a value that taught us that hard work pays off. I also realized that if I was going to hold him captive, and have my own relationship with him, it was going to be through sports. My dad and I went to every Jets game every Sunday and sat in 30-degree weather. My sisters had no interest, and my mother had no interest, so on Sundays, I had him all to myself.

When I think of my childhood, that's what I think of. I think of going to football games with him, and Uncle Leon and Aunt Julie (his brother and sister-in-law).

It was freezing-cold, and my aunt and I would go into the ladies' room at halftime and hold our hands under the blowers for ten minutes.

—Lynn Rosen Karkus

My son Brett plays Division I basketball for the University of Maryland. When he was recruited, it was all my dad talked about for a year. My mother joked that he was going to lose all his friends because he didn't talk about anything else. I said, "It's okay. Let him get joy out of it." His Jewish grandson playing at the highest level of college sports: He loves it!

—Lynn Rosen Karkus

Playing golf with my youngest grandson, Brett Karkus.

Me and Brett.

For as long as I can remember, my grandpa has been as supportive and genuine as they come. He has always been my number-one fan. No one has been more excited and happier about me being a college basketball player than him. When I see people who know my grandpa, they have heard about me. Some of his friends have even joked that they are getting a little tired of hearing about me and my basketball games. But all jokes aside, I am lucky to have been in the presence of a man as great as Martin Rosen, and even luckier to call him my grandpa.

—Brett Karkus

Grandpa Marty does a remarkable job of making each of his great grandkids feel special, and he connects with each one of us on a one-on-one level. He has always been there for me and taken a true interest in everything that I do. We have always bonded over a shared passion for golf. He bought me my first set of golf clubs, and he came to all of my tournaments. His support and positivity has boosted my confidence and made me feel that I can accomplish anything I set my mind to.

—Jason Karkus

Joan, Jason Karkus, and me.

*I consider Grandpa to be one of the true mentors in my life,
someone I could ask advice about life and business.*

—Jason Karkus

Brett Karkus, me, and Jason Karkus.

Everyone loves Marty, Dad, Grandpa, and Great Grandpa!

—Ted Karkus

With my youngest daughter, Nancy.

When I was twelve years old, my dad and I entered the parent-child tennis tournament at the country club. I loved tennis and was excited to play with him. As we were playing the matches, though, some of the parents would slam the ball at me, and we would lose the point. I said to my dad, "Slam the ball back at the kid." I was mad he wouldn't do that. He knew it wasn't the "right" way to win. We won anyway and took home the trophy!

—Nancy Rosen Stern

NANCY

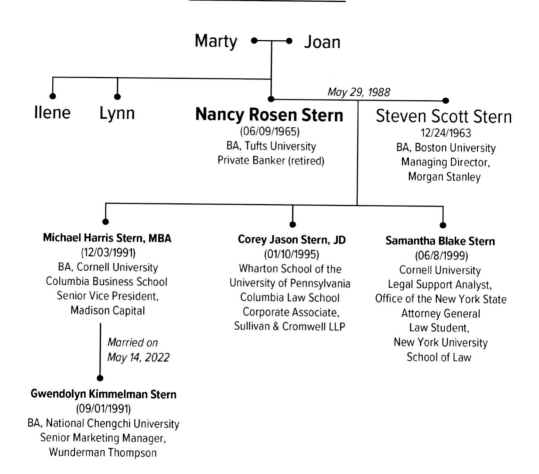

Marty ●━━┓● Joan

Ilene   Lynn

May 29, 1988

Nancy Rosen Stern
(06/09/1965)
BA, Tufts University
Private Banker (retired)

Steven Scott Stern
12/24/1963
BA, Boston University
Managing Director,
Morgan Stanley

Michael Harris Stern, MBA
(12/03/1991)
BA, Cornell University
Columbia Business School
Senior Vice President,
Madison Capital

*Married on
May 14, 2022*

Gwendolyn Kimmelman Stern
(09/01/1991)
BA, National Chengchi University
Senior Marketing Manager,
Wunderman Thompson

Corey Jason Stern, JD
(01/10/1995)
Wharton School of the
University of Pennsylvania
Columbia Law School
Corporate Associate,
Sullivan & Cromwell LLP

Samantha Blake Stern
(06/8/1999)
Cornell University
Legal Support Analyst,
Office of the New York State
Attorney General
Law Student,
New York University
School of Law

One of the most vivid memories I have of my dad is that he came to my school when my little sister Nancy was born— maybe to take me home. I remember being super excited that my dad came to my school!

—Lynn Rosen Karkus

With my grandson Corey Stern at his college graduation.

Education, education, education. My dad was always very involved in my education, and it make me feel supported. My parents took me on college visits to ensure that I attended the best schools for me. Education has always been important to my dad, and he That was always important to my dad, and he imparted that on me and my three children. My oldest son, Michael (31), graduated from Cornell University and Columbia Business School. My middle son, Corey (28), graduated from the University of Pennsylvania and Columbia Law School. My daughter, Samantha (24), graduated from Cornell University and will be attending NYU School of Law (my father's alma mater).

And my parents proudly came to every graduation, from preschool to college (except my daughter's college graduation during COVID, which they watched online).

—Nancy Rosen Stern

Me, Michael Stern, Joan, Samantha Stern, and Corey Stern.

Here we are with all eight of our grandchildren at a family vacation in Mexico. Pictured left to right, top row: Bari Cohen Klein, Michael Stern, Kerri Cohen Saperstein, me, and Joan. Bottom row: Andrew Cohen, Samantha Stern, Corey Stern, Brett Karkus, and Jason Karkus.

I admire that my father has an individual relationship with each one of his eight grandchildren. He is always inquiring about what is going on in their personal lives. Sometimes when I tell him something exciting about one of the kids, he already knows because he speaks to them so frequently.

—Nancy Rosen Stern

Pictured left to right: Steven Stern, me, Michael and Gwen Stern, Nancy Rosen Stern, Joan, Corey Stern, and Samantha Stern at Michael and Gwen's rehearsal dinner.

The first thing I think of when someone asks me about my husband, Michael, is how tight-knit and close everyone in the family is to each other. And I mean close! Marty and Joan don't live more than five minutes from any of their daughters, and it's not out of the ordinary to see Grandpa Marty walking out of the men's card room at Seawane after Michael and I have just finished eating lunch on a Saturday.

Between birthday celebrations, Jewish holidays, and trips to Florida, it became clear early on that family is at the center of everything to my husband, and this special connection stems from his grandparents, Marty and Joan. Grandpa Marty never misses a thing, whether it is taking the grandchildren for trips abroad, making the drives up to camp on visiting day, being there for every college, business school, or law school graduation, and even walking down the aisle at our wedding at 96 years old.

He has created the strongest of bonds among his relatives, something that will transcend generations, and he has instilled a sense of commitment in all his children and grandchildren.

As someone who comes from a family where my relatives are scattered across the world, experiencing firsthand the closeness that exists in the Rosen clan is truly something special.

—Gwendolyn ("Gwen") Kimmelman Stern

Top: Me, Joan, Nancy Rosen Stern, and Steven Stern.

Bottom: Visiting the Stern grandkids at camp. Pictured left to right: Corey, Nancy, Samantha, Joan, me, Steven, and Michael.

I first met Mr. Rosen in January 1986 when I rang his doorbell at 11 p.m. on a Friday night to take his youngest daughter, Nancy, out on our first date. Mr. Rosen opened the door, greeted me very nicely, made no mention of the very late time of night, and then screamed, "Joan, did you see my glasses?" which I noticed were on the top of his head.

This started a 37-year and growing relationship that I value deeply.

He went from "Mr. Rosen" to "Dad" on May 29, 1988, and I have cherished his guidance and mentorship. One of the most important themes that I have taken from Dad is the idea of "family first." He wants to engage with his family as a group and with each person individually. He is genuinely interested in everyone's daily life of school, work, or experiences.

—Steven Stern

Joan and I visited our grandkids at camp whenever we could. Here we are with Samantha Stern.

In the summers, my children attended sleep away camp. My parents insisted on coming to visiting day every year, even when it was hard for them to get around the camp hills. They drove three hours, had to sit in the heat, and then drove another three hours home, but they always showed up. They didn't want to go seven weeks without seeing my kids, and my kids didn't want to go seven weeks without seeing their grandparents.

—Nancy Rosen Stern

When I was younger, I would often stay with my grandparents for a week in the summer while my parents traveled. One summer, I was about four or five years old, and my grandparents took me to see Beauty and the Beast on Broadway. They were so excited and got tickets in the second row. The moment the Beast came on stage, I was terrified and began to cry. I climbed onto my grandpa's lap and sat backwards the entire show. My grandpa joked for years after that he got second-row tickets, and I sat the entire show with my back facing the stage.

—Samantha Stern

In elementary school, whenever I had to choose a hero to write about, I always chose my grandfather (as my brothers and many of my cousins did as well). From a young age, I knew his mark in the world was larger than that of an ordinary grandfather. One of the first times I noticed this was when we all traveled to Los Angeles for the opening of the replica of Simon Wiesenthal's office at the Museum of Tolerance. I couldn't believe that my grandfather was among all of these famous speakers!

He soon realized that we shared a passion for public service. Thus, when the Simon Wiesenthal Center decided to start a government advocacy summer internship program for college students, my grandpa knew it would be a great opportunity for me. A few weeks before my high school graduation I went with him and my grandma to an event for the internship program, hearing then-NYC Public Advocate Letitia James speak.

I vividly recall my grandpa telling me, "You should work for her, she's going places."

The next summer, Letitia James was running for New York State Attorney General. I interned at her NYC Public Advocate's office and worked on her campaign. Now, I am a legal support analyst at the Office of the New York State Attorney General, Letitia James.

I often get calls from my grandpa—"Your boss is on TV!"—and sometimes, he calls about things that she has done that he doesn't agree with.

I have no doubt that my grandfather's influence has had a strong and meaningful impact on my career. One of his biggest pieces of advice to me when embarking on a career in law was that some of the best experience you can get is working in government. He explained that government offices are often resource-strapped and therefore, they give you a lot of responsibility. He is absolutely right.

—Samantha Stern

Top: With granddaughter Samantha Stern, right around the time her back faced the stage.
Left: A more recent picture with Samantha.

Here is the family at my grandson Michael's wedding to Gwen. Left to right, bottom row: Lynn Karkus; Larry and Ilene Cohen; Tyler Klein; Eli Saperstein; Joan and me; and Samantha Stern. Top row: Ted Karkus; Andrew and Liza Cohen; Corey, Steven, and Nancy Stern; Brett Karkus; Michael Stern (the groom), and his beautiful bride, Gwendolyn Kimmelman Stern; Kerri and Eytan Saperstein; Bari, Emma, and David Klein; and Jason Karkus.

A cherished memory with my grandpa is from a few years ago when I moved to the Lower East Side, across the street from the famous Katz's Deli. Grandpa Marty used to tell me stories about how he was related to the family that owned Katz's Deli. When I moved, I called my grandpa up to ask how I could get into Katz's without waiting for hours. Instead of giving me tips, he surprised me by saying that he and my grandma wanted to check out my new apartment and go to Katz's together.

At first, I was skeptical because getting a table at Katz's is almost impossible unless you waited in a line that stretched down the block for an hour plus wait (something my then-94-year-old grandfather wasn't about to do). But, thirty minutes before his arrival, I approached the host and told him my name and that my grandfather was Martin Rosen, who claimed to be cousins with the Katz's founders. To my surprise, the host discovered that my grandpa actually was his third cousin, and my grandfather grew up with his grandfather. He reserved a great corner table for us before we even arrived.

When Grandpa Marty came, we sat down immediately and enjoyed a delicious pastrami on rye sandwich, which cost $25 each. He was shocked at the high price, considering that it used to be just a nickel when he was younger. After dinner, he spoke with the host for 30 minutes, talking about all the cousins in the family, playing the game of Jewish geography. During our lunch, Grandpa Marty took a genuine interest in my personal life, asking me about my work and what was going on in my life. He always makes an effort to connect with each of his grandchildren individually, and this meal at Katz's was just one example of how he demonstrated his love and care for me.

—Michael Stern

With grandson Michael Stern.

The eternal optimist.

Dad's optimism is unmatched in the department of time-management. We were once sitting down to have dinner at Bocaire Country Club when Dad said, "Who wants to see a movie after dinner?"

I told him we wouldn't make it. The movie started in fifteen minutes, and the theater was ten minutes away—and we hadn't eaten yet.

"We will make it," he said. "It's a buffet, and there are previews first."

Sure enough, we finished dinner and walked into the theater just as the movie was starting, though a few of us were a bit nauseated.

We were once on a Rosen family trip in Hawaii headed back to our hotel to watch the New Year's Eve fireworks when Dad said he wanted to stop for a cup of decaf coffee. It was 11:40 p.m. Sure enough, we were able to get a table for eighteen, have coffee, and make it back to the hotel for the start of the fireworks.

—Steven Stern

My dad is an eternal optimist. Steven and my dad used to work a block away from each other, so for family dinners on Monday nights, Steven would ride home with my dad from Manhattan to Long Island, which is about a ninety-minute drive.

My father would call my mother and say, "We will be home in 45 minutes."

My husband would call me and say, "No. We just got in the car. There's no way. We will be home in an hour and a half."

—Nancy Rosen Stern

Me with grandson Corey Stern.

If there is one thing that I admire most about Grandpa Marty, it's his unbridled optimism. He always has a positive attitude, and nothing ever seems to faze him. And because of that, he's lived his life on his own terms.

—Corey Stern

Grandpa Marty retired from practicing law while I was in law school. I've always been in awe of his work ethic, care for his clients, and ability to remain at the top of his game throughout his seventy-year legal career.

However, I'll admit that I found it daunting to think about having to work at that level of intensity for seven more decades. But I think the key to his success was his true passion for his work. You could see how excited he would get when he figured out some creative tax structuring, as well as how much he valued earning the trust and respect of his clients who relied on him when they needed help. It's impressive how many of his clients ended up becoming his friends. He has truly shown by example for his children and grandchildren why it's important to find a career that you love.

—Corey Stern

Joan, Corey Stern, and me at Corey's law school graduation.

FAMILY VACATIONS

have said that work was my focus. Joan was always there for our children, but I was usually at the office. What I lacked in quantity, I tried to make up in quality. At least once a year, I planned a big family trip where I spent as much time with my family as I could. There were no cell phones or emails to check in those days, so I gave my family my full attention.

I cherished those trips, and I kept myself entertained year-round by planning the trip, down to every last detail. I researched restaurants and tourist spots, and I found the best, family-friendly resorts that I knew we would all enjoy.
In the winter of 1975, I was planning to take my family to a resort in Acapulco in Mexico to enjoy a respite from New York winters. I had booked rooms early in the year, and my daughters—who were ten, fifteen, and eighteen at the time—were ready to go.

On a Monday morning in early November, I was reading *The New York Times* when I learned that the United Nations General Assembly had adopted Resolution 3379, which determined that Zionism was a form of racism and racial discrimination. The resolution passed 72 to 35, and it stood until 1991.

Mexico voted in favor.

I said to Joan and the kids, "We are not going to Mexico."

My daughters were devastated.

"But, Daddy, we have been waiting all year for this!"

"I am not going to be democratic about this decision," I said. "I am making the decision for us as a family, and the decision has been made. We are not going to spend any money in a country that says Zionism makes you racist. I am a Zionist. I believe Israel has a right to exist as a protected country. I will not have my money, time, or energy go to a country that says I am racist."

I could not go as a matter of principle. I made many mistakes as a father, but failing to demonstrate principles and conviction would not be one of them.

The next day, I called the rabbi from our temple. I knew the temple was sponsoring a trip to Israel for Christmas, and I asked the rabbi how the plans were coming along.

He informed me that the temple was cancelling the trip because there wasn't enough interest, so the trip was not financially feasible.

"Will you be able to go if five more people join you?"

Turns out, the rabbi needed exactly five more people.

So we went to Israel. The kids were not happy with me at all, but it was a matter of my heart.

Unfortunately, the weather in Israel was horrible. When we arrived, it was dark and dingy. The rabbi went to dinner with us, and after dinner, he and I sat and spoke.

"I envy your trip to Israel," he said.

"Why? You are on the same trip as me."

"I envy your *first* trip to Israel," he said.

What he meant was this: Every person has only one first trip to Israel. The rabbi had already been to Israel many times. But this was my first time experiencing a place where the janitor was Jewish, the restaurant owner was Jewish, police officer outside was Jewish, and the server was Jewish. It was my first time experiencing a country where to be Jewish was normal.

I got to experience my first trip to Israel by giving Joan and our daughters their first trip to Israel. It meant a great deal to me.

Me, Nancy, and Joan in Israel in 2006.

We took a trip to Israel in 2008 for my middle son Corey's bar mitzvah. My dad hired an amazing tour guide, and we toured all day and night. On the last day, at about 5 o'clock, my oldest son (Michael), who was probably sixteen at the time, looked at my dad and said, "Grandpa, can't we just go back and rest a bit before dinner?"

He had said what we were all thinking. But my dad loved to use every minute of every day of our trips. He would tell us, "You'll sleep when we get home."

—Nancy Rosen Stern, our youngest daughter

Here are three generations of Rosens at a family vacation in Jamaica. Pictured left to right, bottom row: Jason Karkus, Andrew Cohen, Corey Stern, Michael Stern, Lynn Karkus, and Brett Karkus. Middle Row: Kerri Cohen Saperstein, Ilene Rosen Cohen, Nancy Rosen Stern, and Joan. Top row: Larry Cohen, Samantha Stern, Steven Stern, me, Bari Cohen Klein, and Ted Karkus.

Grandma and Grandpa have always put family first and have taught us the importance of spending time with family. They put so much time and planning into family vacations, down to every meal, to ensure that we can all spend quality time together. And on every vacation, they are always planning the next trip to look forward to.

But it wasn't just the big family trips—Sunday night dinners at The Seawane Country Club and Monday night dinners at Grandma and Grandpa's house were staples of my childhood. I don't think I ever really appreciated that it wasn't common for other families to all have dinner every week, let alone twice a week!

—Corey Jason Stern, our grandson

Another shot from Jamaica. Pictured left to right, bottom row: Andrew Cohen, Bari Cohen, Corey Stern, and Kerri Cohen. Top row: Joan, Michael Stern, and me.

We have taken many family and extended family trips with my parents over the years (from Jamaica to Mexico to California to London to Israel). My dad planned every detail of the trips, and the dinners were very important to him. He had a folder he carried with him with the entire itinerary and all the reservations. Even though he always worked full time, he wanted to plan each trip to the minute. He spent countless hours on the phone leading up to each trip (as this was before the Internet).

I remember having breakfasts with my parents on Saturday mornings during the summers I was in college. They would be going over their calendars. If Dad's calendar was not full, he was unhappy. He is still like that to this day. He loves to have plans—breakfast, lunch, and dinner.

—Nancy Rosen Stern, our youngest daughter

Pictured left to right, front row: Samantha Stern, Jason Karkus, Joan. Back row: David and Bari Klein, Michael Stern, Corey Stern, me, Andrew Cohen, and Kerri and Eytan Saperstein.

A cruise of the Greek Islands with Joan, our daughters, and our sons-in-law. Left to right: Ted Karkus, Lynn Rosen Karkus, me, Joan, Larry Cohen, Ilene Rosen Cohen, Steve Stern, and Nancy Rosen Stern.

When I think of my grandfather, what initially comes to mind are the life lessons and life stories we heard when we went on our family vacations.

"Luck is what happens when opportunity meets preparation."

"No one can take your education."

"Family first."

These are the pillars of my life, and the foundation came from him and the stories he told us during those family vacations.

—Andrew Cohen, our grandson

My parents loved to travel. They traveled everywhere, with friends and with us.

When we were growing up, my dad was busy. He was young and was building a thriving practice. During the week, he was not home that many nights for dinner. I think this is why family vacations were so important. These vacations were 100-percent family time. We went away every Christmas vacation to Israel, the Caribbean, Hawaii, Mexico, and Florida. When we got older, the trips included the significant others, the grandchildren, the great-grandchildren. It would be twenty-something people, and my dad would plan every detail, down to where we sat at dinner. I think he realized that on a day-to-day basis, he was working, so these vacations were family time. It was more quality than quantity.

One of the most meaningful trips was in 2010 when my little one went to college.

My mom said, "You are an empty-nester now, and you are going to be sad for a bit. Why don't you come with me and Daddy?"

We went to Paris and Normandy. Paris was lovely and beautiful, but to see my dad reliving the war while we were in Normandy was the memorable part. We would go to museums in the morning and stay for twelve hours because he had to see everything about the war and the Holocaust.

And at the end of the day, we would go out for a beautiful dinner. One day after dinner, my dad wanted to go to the casino. The rest of us were exhausted.

I said to my husband, "Larry, you have to go with him. I don't want him to go alone."

And Larry, who is much younger than my dad, did go—but he said, "I can't keep up with him. I am too tired."

He outpaced the rest of us the entire time.

—Ilene Rosen Cohen, our oldest daughter

Family vacations were a big part of growing up in the Rosen household. Even though I loved our trips, as a young girl, I hated the long, fancy dinners we would have when we went to Florida. My dad always made it a point to take me to McDonald's for one meal each trip—just the two of us. I loved our special dates.

—Nancy Rosen Stern, our youngest daughter

Lynn, me, Nancy, and Ilene on a family vacation in 1972.

My son Corey studied abroad in Tel Aviv in 2016 during his junior year at Penn. My husband and I announced during a family dinner that we were going to visit him. My dad pulled his chair up next to us and said, "I want to go. I want to go. I want to go. I want to go to Israel. It could be my last time, and I want to go. I want to go see Corey. I'm coming."

And my mother said to all of us, "No. You're not going. It's dangerous there."

Next thing I knew, my mother said, "I'm coming, too."

My father-in-law also joined us, and we had such a nice trip. We would get back to the hotel at midnight after a long day of touring, and we'd all go straight up to bed—except for my father, who would stay in the lobby for hours, eating ice cream and schmoozing with others.

My dad has an incredible amount of energy.

—Nancy Rosen Stern, our youngest daughter

Me with my grandson Corey Stern in Tel Aviv.

He doesn't like other people to do things that he can do. He has so much competence. Most people would hire a travel agent if they were planning a vacation for twenty people. Not him. Even to this day, he makes every reservation and every arrangement.

He took us on countless trips. He took our entire family to Jamaica and Mexico. He also took my sister and me to Washington, D.C., when we were young. We went on a tour of the White House, and I remember meeting Chris Dodd since he was a friend of my grandfathers. When I turned sixteen, my grandfather, my grandmother, and I went to Venice, Florence, and Rome.

That was such a special trip being that it was just the three of us. He took my immediate family to Israel to Kerri's Bat Mitzvah. He took us all to Las Vegas to visit Uncle Leon. He took us to California. Our family trips were some of my favorite memories growing up.

—Bari Cohen Klein, our granddaughter

Another vacation with the grandkids (minus Brett Karkus, who was a baby).
Front row: Samantha Stern. Middle row: Michael Stern, Corey Stern, and
Jason Karkus. Back row: Me, Bari Cohen Klein, Kerri Cohen Saperstein,
Andrew Cohen, and Joan.

THE MAYOR OF LAWRENCE

For about ten years, nothing in my life happened that was extraordinary. My practice was successful, but I gave limited real contribution to anyone but my family. I was a suburban husband raising three children in the village of Lawrence, which had a population of about 7,000 people.

Before I was born, Lawrence, which is on Long Island, was a WASPy, elegant village—no Jews. About five people ran the village, and none of them were Jewish. And then it started to change.

In 1968, several politicians in Lawrence asked me to run for the Board of Trustees. I ran and was elected. I was one of the first Jewish trustees on the board. I did not identify as a Democrat or a Republican, so it was not a political position. I was responsible for procedural operations. I served two two-year terms, and I suppose I did well because in 1972, I was elected the deputy mayor.

The people on the board were good, decent people. No one cared if you were Jewish, Black, Arab. The mayor was also a prestigious, good man. He was not Jewish, but we had a lot in common. He was a lawyer, and in due time, he became my friend.

In 1976, after being on the board for eight years, I said to him, "I promised my wife I would not do this forever, so it is my time to run for mayor and do what I can do before calling it quits."

He said, "I want to be mayor again."

"You have had many terms."

He said, "Yes, but I want to be mayor again."

"Fine. You are and I friends. I do not want to fight with you. I am going to retire."

"You cannot retire! I need you."

I knew I would win, so I said, "You cannot ask me to stay because you need me and then tell me what I can and cannot do."

We put it to the vote of the Civic Association, and I won.

I enjoyed being mayor. We had typical problems—noise from the airport, issues pertaining to zoning, and managing the staff of fifty or sixty people, but nothing mind-boggling. The job was unpaid and part-time. I came to the meetings at 8 o'clock at night, and the clerk would buy me a corned beef sandwich because I had been working all day.

I would ask him, "What do I owe you?"

He would say, "Mayor, we can pay for it. It's $4."

And I would hand him the $4 and say, "You are not getting me on bribery."

It was a good time. I enjoyed it.

When I run into people from Lawrence, they say, "You used to be mayor 33 years ago. You did a good job."

I did not accomplish everything I wanted to accomplish, though. Lawrence was a bedroom community, meaning there is no industry. It is a residential community. People live there to raise their children, and they work in the cities. The public schools are great, and there is little crime.

But the next town over was becoming different. There were some bigoted people who did not like that it had diversity in its population. When a major hospital wanted to build in Lawrence, the board fought it. They said they didn't want to bring industry into the community. I suspected a number of them didn't want to bring people from the next community into our community.

I said that there should have been an exception for hospitals. We had a heated, year-long debate about whether to give a building permit to the hospital. It was a great hospital, but it was a losing battle. I realized that I was not going to win, so I went along with the majority, and I gave up that battle. I was not proud of that, but I felt I had more to contribute, and I wanted to move forward.

At the end of that four-year term, the village wanted me to run for Congress. Not a chance. I am not a politician. My practice was taking off.

It was a good part of my life, but I retired from politics in 1980 at the age of 55 after my four-year term. I was becoming financially successful, and I had decided it was time to buy a bigger house. Joan found a house that we both loved in Hewlett Harbor, which is one of the towns in the Five Towns Community.

It is a great life. I love the house. My wife loves the house. It is where we have lived ever since, and I am going to die in this house.

We joined the country club, so my kids could swim and play golf. Our lives were provincial. We knew everyone, and they knew us.

I always knew I had to be on good behavior because anywhere I went, people would say, "Oh! You are Marty Rosen's daughter."

There was a high standard we were expected to live up to.

—Ilene Rosen Cohen, our oldest daughter

A family picture at my installation as mayor of Lawrence at Rockhall Museum in 1976. Pictured left to right: Ilene, me, Nancy, Joan, and Lynn.

Growing up, I was always amazed by the fact that no matter where we were—in New York, or Florida, or on vacation somewhere—Grandpa always managed to bump into someone he knew. When he would come to camp visiting days, it felt like all the other kids' grandparents were his friends and clients. He'd have lines of people waiting to talk to him. And in the rare case that we were somewhere, and he didn't know anyone, that never stopped him from working the room. He's the kind of person that can make conversation with someone from any walk of life.

—Corey Jason Stern, our grandson

We have always lived around the corner from my parents. We belong to the same country club and the same temple, and we go to a lot of the same places. My friends love my dad.

When I go out, I always hear, "How's Marty? How's Marty? How's Marty?"

He's a very friendly guy. When we try to leave a restaurant, we cannot get out of there because my dad is going to stop to talk to everyone. He is everyone's friend. Sometimes I will say goodbye to him while we are at the dinner table because I know that as soon as he starts walking out, it will be about a half-hour before he actually walks out the door.

—Nancy Rosen Stern, our youngest daughter

I have many memories of being with Dad at dinner when he says, "Okay, time to go. Let's get up."

For most people, that means putting on their jacket and leaving the restaurant. For Dad, it means we are finished with the eating portion. Nancy and I always estimated that we had at least another 30 minutes before we could give the valet our ticket. Dad would work his way table-to-table toward the door, even stopping to talk with people he never met before. He has an abundance of friends and can fill any size room!

—Steven Stern, our son-in-law

My grandfather is my claim to fame. Anyone I meet says, "Oh, you are Marty Rosen's granddaughter! He is the best. He is the greatest. He is the best tax lawyer! He is the best friend!"

Last year, my husband and I were applying to a country club. We were interviewed over Zoom because it was during the coronavirus pandemic. Before the interview even started,
the man leading the interview told everyone else,
"This is Marty Rosen's granddaughter."

My grandfather isn't even a member of the country club,
but no matter where I go, people love him.

—Bari Cohen Klein, our granddaughter

He is always there for anything we need. He knows the right person to connect us to. He can always help.

When he helped me get jobs when I was younger, I would say, "Oh, Dad. Thank you. This is amazing. I am so lucky."

He would say the same thing to all of us in response, "I didn't get you the job. Luck is when preparation meets opportunity. You were prepared. I opened the door. You had an opportunity, and you ran with it.

—Ilene Rosen Cohen, our oldest daughter

He likes to be extremely social. He would tell my mom: "Call this person. Make a date. Call that person. Make another date."

He likes to be out seven nights a week, and she would be a little more of a home person. It works, but they are a little opposite in that way.

—Ilene Rosen Cohen, our oldest daughter

THE FIRE HYDRANT

Nancy Stern, my youngest daughter

My dad was the mayor of our town, Lawrence, Long Island when I was growing up. I was so proud to be the mayor's daughter! I was happy to accompany him to all his events: meetings, speeches, parades.

In 1976, I was eleven years old, and I noticed that we did not have a fire hydrant on our block. I said to my dad, who was mayor at the time, that he should bring it up at the next village board meeting.

He said, "When the public is invited to speak, why don't you ask for it?"

I practiced and practiced. I had a whole speech prepared. I went to the meeting, which was on a Monday night, and I stood up to speak, but nothing came out of my mouth. Nothing!

I started to cry. So I remember we went home, and my dad practiced with me. We practiced for a whole month. The next month, I went back to the Monday night village board meeting. I asked for my fire hydrant, and I got it!

BOB MCCARTHY

Senior partner at Dentons

G rowing up as a kid in the 1970s, I used to ride my bike in the beauti-ful towns of Lawrence and Hewlett Harbor, villages in Nassau County on Long Island in New York. I did not know it then, but as I was riding through Lawrence, I was riding through the village where Marty Rosen was the mayor at that time.

At that time, Marty was also preparing to visit Germany with his more-like-a-brother friend, Simon Wiesenthal, to press the case for eliminating the statute of limitations on German war crimes. He was also heading the Jewish Documentation Center. He was serving on the board of the Jewish Appeal, and he was running a successful law firm.

Most importantly, together with Joan, he was raising a remarkable, lov-ing, committed family.

If he had stopped at that time, in the 1970s, he would have had a ca-reer and life of stunning significance and consequence. He would have already *made a difference in the lives of individuals in the community. He would have, without exaggeration, made a difference and been of consequence to the whole world.*

But that was not where he stopped. As part of that journey that he was on, Marty had come to Sonnenschein and was part of Dentons. We were honored to be his partners and his friend.

His life and his career are such a testament to the power of goodness—how a life of justice, and a life of love can raise up everybody.

His life brings to mind the words of the prophet Micah. "All that is required of us in life is to act with justice, to love with tenderness, and to walk humbly with our God." (Micah 6:8).

Marty did all of those things, beautifully and with purpose.

PART FIVE

MY BROTHER SIMON

I said earlier that I had a brother. Leon was fifteen months older than me. He was born on May 21, 1924, and he died in 2015 at the age of ninety. Though we were close in age, Leon and I were about as different as night and day. I loved him as much as I could love a person. He was fun and kind. He had no children of his own, but he loved my children as his own, and they loved him in return. He married a lovely woman named Juliet who died in 2010 at the age of ninety-five. They were happy, and I believe they lived a full life together.

Leon was an amazing brother. He was a constant, and I never had a single complaint about him. I mean no disrespect to Leon when I say that I had a second brother, Simon Wiesenthal.

I already told you a bit about Simon. I won't include his entire life story because Simon wrote his own books, including *The Murderers Among Us, The Sunflower,* and *Justice, Not Vengeance*. You, like some historians, will note inconsistencies in this book. He writes that he was in eleven concentration camps; history says he was in "just" five.

On these inconsistencies, I will say, so what? Simon lived through more trauma than any man should have to. If you cannot understand that his memories were often fragmented and tortured, then to that I say, count your blessings. Those of us who have seen war are not so lucky. Simon's mother, Rosa, was killed in Belzec, an extermination camp designated to murder all Polish Jews as part of the Final Solution. Simon once said that he hoped Rosa died on the train to Belzec because the other option was that she died in a gas chamber. Can you imagine not knowing whether your mother died alone, scared, and starving in a cattle car, or in a gas chamber—and having to decide that the first scenario is the one that gives you more comfort?

As to the number of concentration camps in which he was imprisoned, I say this: If you should wish to argue with me about whether the forced labor camps constituted "concentration camps," and whether the Nazis can be relied upon to generate an exact roster of transfers, then you and I are fighting a different war. One concentration camp is one too damn many.

Some have called Simon a liar; others have called him a traitor. I call him my brother. I knew him for forty years, so I knew his flaws and his virtues better than anyone.

Simon Wiesenthal was the most honorable man I have ever known.

His wife, Cyla, once told him that she felt like he was married not only to her, but also to six million Holocaust victims. My wife asked him why he committed his life to something that tortured him, and he responded by saying that a soldier stays on the battlefield.

It wasn't just the Jews that Simon defended. Simon sought justice for the Jehovah's Witnesses, Roma and Sinti, Poles, Blacks, gays and lesbians, and the disabled who were murdered in the Holocaust. At a memorial ceremony honoring Simon's life, the then-United Nations Secretary General Kofi Annan credited Simon for strengthening his conviction that the United Nations needed "to remain at the center of the world's struggle for human rights and human dignity," attributing him with the paving the way for countries like Rwanda and the former Yugoslavia to bring justice for war crimes, and for world leaders to fight genocide and ethnic cleansing.[4]

"As Simon Wiesenthal himself might well have said, we cannot just consign this evil to the past and forget about it," said General Annan. "Every generation must be on its guard. As survivors such as Simon die, it falls to us to carry forward the work of remembrance."

To me, the lesson of Simon Wiesenthal is that one person—if they want to and if they try—can make a difference. He made a difference. Bearing witness to his efforts was the honor of my life.

Simon truly was family, not just to me, but also to Joan and my daughters.
We often traveled to visit each other's families and spent holidays
together. He knew my kids, and I was and am quite fond of his daughter,
Paulinka. Pictured: Joan and Simon.

4   Annan, K. (2005, September 28). Secretary-general, in remarks at Memorial Ceremony, says Wiesenthal convinced him of need to keep United Nations at centre of Struggle for Human Rights, dignity | UN press. United Nations. Retrieved May 4, 2023, from https://press.un.org/en/2005/sgsm10131.doc.htm

U.S. OFFICE OF WAR CRIMES

As I told you earlier, Simon kept a list of Nazi criminals while he was imprisoned in numerous camps. While at Mauthausen, he aided the United States military in interrogating Nazis. In due time, he began working for the U.S. Office of War Crimes in tracking down Nazis. He moved into a small schoolhouse that had been converted into a home for survivors of the Holocaust. The home, which was in Leonding, Austria, looked out onto a cemetery that bore the headstones of Alois and Klara Hitler.

Simon quickly put in for a transfer and relocated to a small apartment near the U.S. Office of War Crimes in Linz. In the summer of 1945, he found an attorney whom he knew before the war. The attorney helped him send word to Warsaw alerting Cyla that he was still alive. After three years of not knowing whether the other had survived, Simon and Cyla were reunited.

In due time, the political landscape began changing. The Nuremberg Trials in 1945 and 1946 convicted 161 Nazis and sentenced 37 of them to death. Fewer and fewer countries were investigating Nazi war crimes.

With little to no money, Simon started minor investigations to find Nazi war criminals on his own. Often, other citizens would help him; partisans would assist in looking for little guys—not the big Nazis like Eichmann. Remember, Simon had no money and no relatives. He had little but his virtues.

Nonetheless, Simon began to build these investigations, and he became influential. He received a few handouts from Western European governments, such as England and France.

In the early 1960s, Simon became involved in part of the Adolf Eichmann case. Eichmann was the major Nazi. He was one of the Nazi leaders who planned to implement the "Final Solution to the Jewish Question," and he was the person who managed the logistics of the genocide of six million Jewish people. He was captured in 1945 by the Allied Forces, but he escaped to Argentina and spent the next fifteen years as a free man.

In 1960, Eichmann was hiding out in Buenos Aires. Simon learned information about his whereabouts and handed that over. Coupled with other evidence, this helped the Mossad find Eichmann. He was captured, tried by the Israeli Supreme Court, convicted, and executed in Ramla in 1962.

In due time, though, Simon stopped receiving the money necessary to hunt Nazis. The war was over, Eichmann had been caught, and countries were not prioritizing the capture of Nazis anymore. Simon was living in Vienna at the time. He decided to travel to the United States in search of Holocaust survivors—men and women with the Nazi tattoo on their left forearm—and ask them to help fund his efforts.

Simon later told me that most people offered to give him $5 or $10. They didn't want to think about it anymore.

Simon decided, "Time to quit. I cannot fight this on my own."

This was 1965. He and his wife had started a family, so he figured he would go to Israel and live out his life.

Fortunately, an English newspaper in Tokyo ran an article announcing that Nazi hunter Simon Wiesenthal was closing up his shop in Vienna and moving to Israel. My friend and client, Herman Katz, who was a hunter of lions and tigers, read that article. He picked up the phone and called Simon.

"Mr. Wiesenthal, you do not know me. My name is Herman Katz. I see that you are quitting. Why?"

"It's very simple. I have no money. Nobody cares."

"I care. Do not quit."

Herman went on to tell Simon that he will fly to Vienna to have dinner with him the next night.

Herman told Simon over dinner: "I do not know how we will do this, but the world needs you. I need you. Someone needs to be accountable for these monsters."

Herman gave Simon a check for under $10,000. Herman then came back to the United States, where he met with his lawyer. That lawyer was me. In addition to being a hunter of lions and tigers, Herman was in the garment industry, and I represented him.

He explained that he wanted my help establishing a foundation to help Simon, which I and others assisted.

We created the Jewish Documentation Center, which I eventually ended up running, and which existed to help find Nazis and bring them to justice.

The post office eventually refused to deliver to my office on Fifth Avenue while I was running the Jewish Documentation Center. I received too many threatening letters, and the other tenants were afraid that someone would bomb the place. Too many people were actively pro-Nazi and anti-Jewish.

In 1982, Simon's own home was bombed by a handful of German and Austrian neo-Nazis. Simon and Cyla, who were asleep in their bed,

*were unharmed. During the trial, one of the neo-Nazis punched Simon
and knocked him to the floor. Simon stood up, wiped his hands, combed
his hair, and testified.*

*Simon did not let people scare him away from doing what he
believed was the right thing, and I have done my best to live a life that
follows his great example.*

Over the next thirty years, Simon became a brother to me. He used to
say that he had 89 relatives die in the Holocaust, and he had a right to name
someone as a brother. I felt the same way. He loved me, and he loved my family.
He went to my kids' bat mitzvahs and their weddings. I never dreamed in my life
that I would have exposure to this.

Herman, Simon, and I would meet in a kosher restaurant, Lou G. Siegel,
in New York City to discuss the cases that Simon was working on. My job was to
make sure he was following the law and reasonable in action.

I must confess, there were times when it was not easy. Remember, we
were hunting Nazis. We were dealing with people who were just horrific. And
there would come a time when someone—it was usually Herman—would say,
"Kill him! I want him dead."

There were times when Herman wanted to hire extermination squads.
And who could blame him? We could cut these monsters into tiny pieces, and it
would never be enough to give justice for what the Nazis did. But we all knew,
once you start acting like them, you become them.

Simon would say, "We won't kill anyone. If we kill them, we are as bad
as they are. And we do not want to kill them. We want to try them, so the papers show the world what happened. I want the world to know there was a
Holocaust."

Simon was clear in his goals. He wanted to bring Nazi war criminals to justice and leave a historical record of what these animals had done.

That is what we did. Over the course of many years together, Simon helped capture 1,100 Nazis, including Franz Stangl, the head of the Treblinka concentration camp, who murdered about 750,000 Jews. Just around the corner from me on Long Island, he found Hermine Braunsteiner, who was living as Hermine Ryan, a housewife. Hermine supervised the killing of several hundred Jewish children in Majdanek. Thanks to Simon, she was extradited to Germany for trial as a war criminal and received life imprisonment. I once hired a Paraguayan pilot to fly to Paraguay to look for Josef Rudolf Mengele, the doctor who performed experiments on prisoners in Auschwitz. Mengele was already dead, but we did not know that. It was crazy what he was accomplishing.

In 1958, neo-Nazis and Holocaust deniers began saying that Anne Frank was a fictitious character—that the Jews made up her story to garner sympathy. Simon was incensed, and he figured that if he could track down the Nazi who arrested the Frank family, he could defeat the neo-Nazi propagandists. It took Simon five years, but he tracked down Karl Silberbauer, who was working as a police officer in Vienna.

He was exonerated, with the courts deciding that his actions did not rise to the level of war crimes. But everyone knows: Karl Silberbauer is the man who arrested fourteen-year-old Anne Frank and sent her to her death.

We did not go after everyone, though. From 1972 until 1981, the Secretary-General of the United States was an Austrian named Kurt Waldheim. In 1986, he ran for president of Austria, where it became known that he served as an intelligence officer for Nazi Germany during World War II. People accused Waldheim of being guilty of Nazi crimes, and they called for Simon, as the voice of justice for Holocaust victims, to condemn Waldheim. Simon researched the case, and he refused to condemn Waldheim, who, in turn, became the Austrian president.

Simon's refusal stems from the fact that Waldheim's conduct did not elevate to a war crime. Waldheim was a lieutenant junior grade who worked in Crete processing papers. He did not personally put people into ovens. Simon's distinction was that filing papers was not a Nazi crime.

He believed that he needed to have certainty when accusing someone of a Nazi war crime—and that if the standards were not exceedingly high for making that accusation, his efforts and his reputation would be watered down.

His explanation was, "If I accuse every German of being a Nazi, then the work I do is useless because I have no value of discerning what is important and what is not important."

You cannot lock up one million Germans.

THE SIMON WIESENTHAL CENTER

U nbeknownst to us, a rabbi named Marvin Hier wanted to form an organization in the North American hemisphere to pursue the Nazis. Rabbi Hier had met Simon years prior when he visited Vienna while working as a rabbi at the oldest synagogue in Vancouver, Congregation Schara Tzedeck. Simon had kindly spent some time with the rabbi when he had unexpectedly knocked on the door of Simon's office in the late 1960s or early 1970s.

The meeting had been friendly, but nothing came of it.

Years later, the rabbi contacted Simon. He had an idea. He wanted to form a Los Angeles-based Jewish human rights organization in Simon's name. The rabbi was persistent about meeting with Simon, who eventually asked me to step in.

"I like this idea," Simon told Rabbi Hier. "Will I agree to it? That depends on my lawyer."

"Who is your lawyer?" asked Rabbi Hier.

"Martin Rosen of Rosen & Reade in New York."

Simon called me: "The next time you are in Los Angeles, please see this rabbi on Pico Boulevard. He has a yeshiva, and he keeps hounding us to form an organization in my name with him. I told him that you are our friend and lawyer, and without your consent, we will not do it."

By coincidence, I had a business meeting in Los Angeles two months later, so when I landed in Los Angeles, I called the yeshiva.

When a man answered, I said abruptly, "Who is this?"

He responded, "Who is this?"

I said, "I asked you first."

He said, "Who is this."

I told you he was persistent. I said, "I am Martin Rosen. If you are Rabbi Hier, we are supposed to meet."

"Yes, I want to meet you."

I took a taxi to his office, which I thought would be a big office for the yeshiva. Instead, it was a humongous room with two chairs and a little table.

We spent four hours talking. I called Simon back and said, "This guy is a winner."

That is how the Simon Wiesenthal Center in Los Angeles was formed, and I sit on the board to this day. We had a meeting just last month, and Rabbi Hier told that story—that the Simon Wiesenthal Center would not have started without my endorsement.

I knew he was a winner, and I was right. By my estimation, Rabbi Hier is the most prominent rabbi in the world, and I am proud to call him my friend. I remind him often that I discovered him, but the credit goes to Rabbi Hier. He is brilliant.

Today, the Simon Wiesenthal Center has over 400,000 member families helping to defend Jews and teach the lessons of the Holocaust. It has offices in Los Angeles, New York, Chicago, Miami, Toronto, Paris, Jerusalem, and Buenos Aires, and it includes a film division (Moriah Films), which has one two

Academy Awards. It also includes the Museum of Tolerance in Los Angeles, and the Museum of Tolerance in Jerusalem, which is opening this year.

Top: Rabbi Hier, Joan, and me.

Left: Me and Simon, with Rabbi Hier behind Simon's shoulder. I believe this is from the late 1980s or early 1990s at the Simon Wiesenthal Center.

Speaking at the dedication of the new facility at the Simon Wiesenthal Center in Los Angeles. Seated in the front row are former California governors Gray Davis and Arnold Schwarzenegger, as well as then-mayor Antonia Villaraigosa.

THE LA BREA TAR PIT MUSEUM

Contributed by Rabbi Marvin Hier, dean and founder of the Simon Wiesenthal Center and the Museum of Tolerance and author of Meant to Be: A Memoir. Excerpts from Meant to Be used with the permission of The Toby Press.

O ne day, my wife and I took our children to the La Brea Tar Pit Museum in Los Angeles. The tar pits are a paleontological research and excavation site. The museum preserves the bones of animals that are discovered as the natural asphalt rises to the surface.

On that day, a young child visiting the tar pits asked the museum's docent this question: "Could the dinosaurs come back?"

The docent responded by explaining that dinosaurs could not come back because climate conditions on planet Earth have changed such that dinosaurs could not survive.

On the drive home with my wife and two children, I asked my wife, "What if we were to ask the same question, but we substituted Hitler for dinosaurs. Could Hitler come back? Would our answer be the same as the docent's answer to that young child's question?"

My wife and I both agreed: No, we could not give the same answer as *the docent did. The planet is still full of hatred and bigots, and we would not say that the Holocaust could never happen again.*

I could not let it go—this idea that the United States should be doing more to protect Jewish human rights.

I made a call, or several calls, to Simon, who agreed to meet me in Vienna. During that meeting, I explained that I wanted to create a Holocaust center in America and name it in Simon's honor.

"Look, this is for me very strange," said Simon. "What can I say? I am honored. I did not expect this. Nobody has ever come to Vienna to ask me for my name. Usually they come to give me the name of a Nazi they want me to hunt down. But you must understand: I am a Nazi hunter, not a teacher. I agree that what you want to do is right. But millions died and thousands like me survived. We were all in the camps together. Why pick only one name for your building?"

"Because Mr. Wiesenthal," I responded. "You are the only man who has never moved on. Instead, you stayed behind, looking at that map, day after day, spending every moment pursuing justice for the millions who were killed. Mr. Wiesenthal, all the survivors will agree that your name deserves to be on our building."

After a long pause, he responded.

"Look, I must say, I like the idea. For years, whenever I have gone to America to speak, I have asked survivors why they don't create an institution to teach about the Holocaust. They have promised me many times they will do something. But still today there is absolutely nothing. I like also that you are an activist who wants to speak out about anti-Semitism. I have always said anybody can do research, but the question is what you do with the research. If you store it away like food in a freezer, it is rarely used. If you publish it in journals, it only reaches the intellectuals. Today, the fight against the haters must be taken to the public. After all, it is a fight to protect our children and grandchildren and future generations against a repetition of those crimes. Look, what can I tell

you? I'm impressed. But I need to know more before I give you a final answer. I am going to send my lawyer and friend, Martin Rosen, to Los Angeles to meet with you. After that, I will let you know what I decide."

When Marty met with me, I had just purchased a building to start what would become the Yeshiva University High School of Los Angeles. The building was empty, and I do not believe it had electricity yet.

Still, I convinced him.

"Hatred is all over the place," I remember Marty saying to me. "I am going to encourage Simon to agree to your idea. I can see from your enthusiasm that you are not going to give up, which is what I like about you."

To this day, I remind him: If not for Marty Rosen, the Simon Wiesenthal Center would not have existed.

Simon Wiesenthal's speech at the inauguration of the Simon Wiesenthal Center
November 22, 1977

"Most people have no idea how many Jews we have lost over the past 2,000 years. Among the sixty million inhabitants of the Roman Empire, there were four million Jews, half a million of whom lived in ancient Israel, the rest in Italy, Spain and other parts of the Empire. At this same time, the British Isles held about one million people; today more than fifty million live there. If the Jews had been left to develop like the British, there would be two hundred million Jews in the world today. However, we are only fourteen million.

Why? Because we are the leftovers of pogroms, inquisitions, and Hitler. It was not only mass slaughter, but also forced baptisms and voluntary escape from Judaism, which took its toll on our numbers.

Whenever I speak, people tell me, "I have not lost anybody in the Holocaust. I am not a survivor." This is why I always tell my audiences that it is my firm belief that the Jews in America—whether they formerly had been living in Europe, whether they had lost relatives in the Holocaust or not—are all survivors. Every Jew alive today is a survivor! If Hitler had won the war, the first thing he would have said to the defeated nation is: "Give me your Jews!"—just as he had done all over Europe. And in each and every country, he would have found people ready to give up the Jews. It is only because Hitler lost the war that there are still Jews alive."

—an excerpt from *Meant to Be,* Rabbi Hier's memoirs, and used with the permission of The Toby Press

Rabbi Hier, Joan, and me.

THE GERMAN BUNDESTAG

n January of 1979, Simon called me and told me something I did not know: The German statute of limitations on war crimes was set to expire on December 31 of that year. What this meant was that anyone could come out on January 1, 1980, and say, "I killed 200,000 Jews," and they could be handed a medal and given a reward.

In most countries, including the United States, there is no statute of limitations for murder or genocide, but Germany was the exception.
Simon called me and said, "How do we stop this?"

I am a practical person. I said to Simon, "Look, we cannot stop this. Who are the people that killed the Jews? They are Germans. The average age of a Nazi back in 1940 to 1945 was twenty or twenty-five. In 1979, the Nazis were primarily about 45 to 55 years old. And how old do you think most members of the Bundestag [the German cabinet] are? About 45 to 55 years old."

"We cannot stop this," I told Simon. "No one will vote for the abolition of the statute of limitations. There are surely Nazis in the Bundestag, or brothers, cousins, or friends of Nazis."

I was wrong.

Across Germany, we distributed a postcard for people to sign and send to Chancellor Schmidt, asking him to abolish the statute of limitations on German war crimes. The postcard showed an SS soldier holding a gun and whip to a prisoner's head, while two other prisoners hung from trees. The back of the postcard read: "This murderer has not been found! He and thousands of other Nazi criminals, living free, many under aliases, are waiting for December 31, 1979, when, under the current law, their crimes will fall under the statute of limitations."

To this day, I have no idea if anyone signed or sent the postcard. It probably cost a quarter to return it, so maybe not.

But word got to the German government that people were objecting, and the Chancellor of Germany—a great man named Helmut Heinrich Waldemar Schmidt—said, "We have decided not to take an official position on this case. I want the Bundestag to vote their conscience. This a matter of conscience for the country of Germany, determining whether what we did was right or wrong."

He further decided to invite a representative group to come to the German capital. They would discuss the issue with the Bundestag. He did not have to do that, but he handled it fairly. If he did not, we would have lost, automatically.

"Would you come to Germany?" asked Rabbi Hier.

I had never been busier in my entire life. I was then the mayor of Lawrence, N.Y. I had three children. I had a busy practice, and I had a wife who did not like when I traveled for work to Boston, much less to Germany. Beyond that, I hated Germany. I had been there as a soldier in World War II, and I did not want to go back.

"No. Since the war, I have hated Germany," I told the rabbi.

I returned home that night, and Joan said, "You should go. It is important, and this means a lot to you."

A few other people were traveling to Germany from New York. One was Chris Dodd, a congressman who was running for Senate. Another was Bayard Rustin, a Black civil rights leader. I remember getting on a call with Rabbi Hier and saying, "I will not travel on Lufthansa Airlines."

Lufthansa was founded by Deutsche Luft Hansa, which had ties to the Nazi party. I was a Jewish man, and I was not going to step foot on Lufthansa. Rabbi Hier said, "Go with Chris Dodd and Rustin. They are good men. You will be okay."

I got a call from them, so I changed my ticket, and we went together. We flew into Munich, where we all met with the Israeli ambassador to Germany, who wanted to discuss our plan and share with us what he knew about the German way of thinking. I remember that someone used an idiom that was a racial slur against Blacks, and I apologize to Bayard that he had to hear it, particularly while he was advocating for human rights issues.

Bayard was very distinguished, and he had a great sense of humor about him. He responded with, "That's okay. As long as he didn't call me a *shvartzer!*" We became friends, and the next day, we traveled to Bonn, which is the secondary seat of the Chancellor and the Bundestag.

The sixth day that we were there, a television program called Holocaust was broadcast, and the television station that played the program was bombed. But the television station did the right thing, and it played the program the next day.

This was while we were having meetings with the Bundestag! One of the members of the Bundestag was the son of Claus von Stauffenberg, a Germany army officer and resistance leader who was killed after several failed attempts to assassinate Hitler, Heinrich Himmler, and Hermann Göring.

Even though his father had been killed by Hitler, Franz-Ludwig Schenk Graf von Stauffenberg did not want to abolish the statute of limitations. He had that German attitude of, "The law is the law is the law. You never change it."

We stayed for days. We went to many meetings. We debated. We thought they were crazy; they thought we were crazy. And I remember seeing that the members of the Bundestag were all relatively young and saying, "We don't stand a chance."

There were 500 members of the Bundestag, and we needed a majority. On the last day, they took the vote.

We won by 23 votes. That's it. If twelve people had voted the other way, today, 44 years after that vote, anyone could stand up in Germany and say, "I killed 100,000 Jews."

It would not be illegal. And they could keep killing Jews thereafter.

It's amazing that we stopped that from happening, and to this day, I still don't know how we did it. A man was tried a year ago in German for being a Nazi: 101-year-old Josef Schütz. He was an accomplice in the murder of 3,518 people. We know his name, and we are recording it in the books of history that Josef Schütz was a Nazi and a murderer.

More importantly, our work with the German Bundestag stopped the issue. Let me explain. In most countries, including Germany and the United States, you cannot pass an ex-post-facto bill, meaning you cannot outlaw something that has already been done. You cannot say, "We will make it illegal to have done something in the past."

So if it was no longer illegal to kill Jews in the Holocaust, what would preclude people in 1981 from going out and killing Jews as part of the Holocaust efforts?

Nothing! They could have killed Jews with impunity. We stopped that from happening.

Most people did not know what really occurred in World War II. You have to remember that when the war was over, people saw one or two pictures of what happened in Auschwitz and the big camps, but most people did not know the immensity of the killing.

When I give speeches, I give this analogy.

Today, you read the paper in cities, and you read that ten people are killed, sometimes twenty people: women and men and children. Every day! When you read these stories, you feel three things:

Emotion #1: Surprise. How could you kill ten kids?

Emotion #2: Sympathy. I feel sorry for the family.

Emotion #3: Justice. Was he apprehended?

Those are your three emotions for non-Holocaust murders.

Now let's go to the Holocaust. You learn that six million Jews were killed. Six million! That's a big surprise. And you feel great remorse for their families.

Now what about apprehension?

Zero. Zero.

And why? They killed six million Jews. We know that twenty million people were killed in the Russian front. And we know that gays, Jehovah's Witnesses, Roma and Sinti, Poles, Blacks, and the disabled were also rounded up and killed by the Nazis. How many were killed by the Empire of Japan? Maybe fifty or seventy-five million people were killed in World War II. It's incredible.

Now think about how many people it took to kill all those people. Who was going to apprehend all the people responsible?

Nobody. The most famous legal cases were the Nuremberg Trials held in 1945 and 1946, and they only sentenced only twenty-four Nazis to death. That's it.

How can you find the people responsible for the death of fifty to seventy-five million people from the day Hitler invaded Poland on September 1, 1939, until the war ended?

Everybody wanted to go home to their family, go back to living.

What we did, it is extraordinary. But it was not me. I want to make that clear. It was my friend Rabbi Hier. It was Dodd and Rustin, and it was Simon Wiesenthal.

Nobody knows what they did. If you talk to people on the streets about World War II, they do not know that there was a statute of limitations on war crimes. They do not know that this debate and victory in Germany led to justice for victims of war crimes in Rwanda and Yugoslavia. They do not know that the United Nation's approach to genocide and ethnic cleansing changed because of Simon, Rabbi Hier, and the German Bundestag.

It is not written up in the history books, but it happened. I was there.

Then-Senator Chris Dodd (D-CT), Simon, and me in Germany in 1979 to fight the expiration of the statute of limitations on war crimes.

JEALOUSY

During the course of our friendship, Simon told me—and others—that in the 1950s, he went to the World Jewish Council to let them know that he had information about the whereabouts of Adolf Eichmann. Simon had no money, so he asked the World Jewish Council for $500 to continue pursuing the case.

The short story was this: Adolf Eichmann's parents lived not far away from Simon's apartment, which at the time was in Linz. Simon convinced the U.S. Office of War Crimes to search the Eichmann household and question his parents. They found nothing—not even a picture of Eichmann. But Simon learned that Eichmann's wife, Veronica, and their children were living near a lake in a beautiful town called Altausee in Austria. Rumors were circulating that Eichmann was there, too. Despite efforts to get information, Wiesenthal failed to locate Eichmann.

Simon never stopped thinking of Adolf Eichmann. Eventually, the stress of hunting Nazis was causing a toll on his health, so he began collecting stamps as a hobby. A fellow stamp collector was an Austrian baron who disclosed to Simon that he received a letter from someone in Argentina who met and knew Eichmann.

Wiesenthal took this information to the World Jewish Council. He explained that he would be able to collect Eichmann's address, but he needed $500 to hire someone who spoke Spanish to travel to Argentina and investigate.

The World Jewish Council, which was a major organization, turned Simon's request down.

Eichmann was not apprehended until 1962, and Simon played a role in that. Over the years, he learned that Veronica had moved to Buenos Aries and was living with a man named Karl Clemens. But with no pictures of Eichmann, Simon could do little to provide evidence that Clemens and Eichmann were the same person. This was before Internet and cell phones. Finding people required much more work.

When Eichmann's father died, Simon sent a photographer to take pictures of Eichmann's siblings. His brother bore a striking resemblance to Karl Clemens.

This picture played a small role in helping the Mossad identify and capture Eichmann in Buenos Aires.

It always angered Simon that the World Jewish Council had not done more. When the Mossad finally captured Eichmann, Simon publicly criticized the World Jewish Council.

General Counsel for the World Jewish Council was a fellow named Eli Rosenbaum. Rosenbaum invariably liked to knock Simon as a phony and a fraud. You wouldn't think that people would do that, but they do. Anybody who arrests one Nazi is a hero—and that includes Rosenbaum. Rosenbaum did not see it that way, though. Simon was known worldwide as the conscience of the Holocaust, and I suppose Rosenbaum was jealous.

Eventually, Rosenbaum became the director of the Office of Special Investigations of the Department of Justice. His main job was identifying and deporting Nazi war criminals. It was a terrific program, and over the course of twenty-five years, Rosenbaum apprehended many Nazis.

The Simon Wiesenthal Center apprehended 1,100—and to this day, the work Simon did with Rabbi Hier continues to chip away at war crimes, genocide, and ethnic cleaning, bringing a measure of justice for the victims of the Holocaust.

Oddly, Rosenbaum took issue with Simon. It started when Rosenbaum wrote a book alleging the betrayal of Kurt Waldheim, the president of Austria. In that book, Rosenbaum also alleged that Simon had betrayed the Jewish people by refusing to name Waldheim as a war criminal.

Rabbi Hier read the book.

"What is your opinion?" the rabbi asked me.

I am not a very hardened person, but I can be tough if I need to be. I have compassion for people, particularly people who have been the subject of bigotry or racism, but on that day, I found no compassion for Rosenbaum.

I loved Simon Wiesenthal.

I said, "Let's sue him."

The rabbi, who is a great and brilliant man, had a different idea in mind.

"If we sue him, people will read the book," said the Rabbi. "If we do not, no one will read the book."

The rabbi was right. I wanted vengeance; the rabbi directed me toward justice.

We did not sue Rosenbaum, but I was angry. To me, Simon's work was a matter of love and justice. It was not a lot of justice—it was six million versus 1,100. But it was some justice. It was something.

That Rosenbaum was attacking Wiesenthal felt like more injustice added on top of a pile of dead Jewish bodies.

Shortly before Simon died, he received the Freedom from Fear Award from the Roosevelt Institute, which was established in Holland to carry forth the policies of Franklin and Eleanor Roosevelt. Simon was chosen "for compelling us to remember that barbaric horror of Nazism and thus help to ensure that it will not be repeated and for dedicating his life to justice not vengeance."

In 1941, then-president Franklin Roosevelt described his four freedoms, stating: "The fourth is freedom from fear — which, translated into world terms, means a world-wide reduction of armaments to such a point and in such a thorough fashion that no nation will be in a position to commit an act of physical aggression against any neighbor —anywhere in the world."

For Simon to receive this award from the president who sought to liberate prisoners from concentration camps was monumental. The Four Freedoms were conceived of when Simon was living in a forced labor camp in Soviet-occupied Russian. Simon would never forget that it was Americans who liberated him. He would remember until his dying day spotting the American flag while he was on all four knees eating blades of grass to nourish his emaciated body.

An award from the Roosevelt Institute! This should have been a moment of pure honor and joy.

I was invited to attend the awards ceremony in Holland as Simon's guest. When the award is presented to Americans, it is presented in New York City. To non-Americans, such as Simon, the award is presented in Middleburg, which is the capital of Zeeland in the Netherlands.

Simon was given the award by the Queen of Holland, Beatrix of the Netherlands.

While he was in Middleburg, though, Simon became very ill—so ill that it eventually sent him to the hospital. He was an old man, and Rosenbaum had just come after him again, attacking Simon as a fraud.

In a broadcast that appeared in a German newspaper, written in German, Rosenbaum accused Simon of colluding with the Nazis, which of course was ridiculous. The broadcast included four pictures of the United States Justice Department, which is where Rosenbaum worked. Those photos made it appear that the U.S. Justice Department was investigating Simon for Nazi crimes.

I wrote a scathing letter to Rosenbaum. How dare he criticize the man who spent his whole life hunting Nazis! How jealous must he be! I really let him have it.

He never answered me.

Meanwhile, Simon ended up in the hospital. His body was sickened that people could say these things about him and the cause.

When I learned that Simon was in the hospital, I was at home lamenting to my wife about my anger. I got tired of complaining, and I decided to do something, so I picked up the phone and started making phone calls to the United States Justice Department.

After ten phone calls, I finally got someone to give me a phone number of a Department of Justice official. His name was Robert Litt.

I said to myself, *I know this guy.* He had previously been an attorney in New York and, in fact, represented one of my clients. He clerked for judges first, and then he ended up being the U.S. attorney for the Southern District of New York. At that point, he was working as a deputy assistant attorney general with Janet Reno under the Clinton Administration.

When I got Litt on the phone, I said, "Bob, this is Marty Rosen."

"Marty Rosen? How the heck are you, my friend!"

"Bob, you have known me a long time. Sit with me. I need your help."

I explained to Litt what was happening, and he was shocked that anyone would allege Simon to be a neo-Nazi.

"I have the tape," I said to my friend, Bob.

"Send me the tape. If what you are saying is right, I will do something about it."

Litt called me a few weeks later.

"It's terrible," he said of the broadcast. "What do we do?"

"I want him fired."

"If we get him fired, I am afraid that the Senate will not continue to fund the Office of Special Investigations for hunting Nazis. Is that what you want?"

I did not want that. I wanted Simon's name cleared, but I also wanted Rosenbaum to continue doing his work with the Office of Special Investigations.

I did not know what to do, so I called Senator Chris Dodd, who said, "I have a great idea. Janet Reno is going to make a speech on Yom HaShoah [Holocaust Remembrance Day], and she will apologize."

Reno did not apologize. She said she would, but she most certainly did not.

Dodd's next call was to President Bill Clinton, who wrote a formal apology. And on August 9, 2000, President Clinton awarded Simon with the Presidential Medal of Freedom.

Simon was the only Jew getting a presidential medal that day, and he was the only non-citizen. He was too ill to travel to the Rose Garden, so Rabbi Hier and I traveled to Washington, D.C. The rabbi accepted the honor on Simon's behalf.

This is the statement from the White House:

"A survivor of World War II concentration camps, Simon Wiesenthal has been at the forefront of Holocaust remembrance for more than 50 years, devoting his life to bringing perpetrators of Nazi atrocities to justice. His efforts have ensured the arrest of more than 1,000 war criminals, and he continues to inspire others in the fight against racism and intolerance.

"For his commitment to preserving the memory of Holocaust victims, his unrelenting pursuit of truth, and his dedication to educating a new generation about the devastating conse-

*quences of remaining silent in the face of horror, the world
owes its profound gratitude to Simon Wiesenthal."*

For Simon to receive that honor was another small piece of justice.

*Simon was awarded the Presidential Medal of Freedom on August 9, 2000. Rabbi Hier
and I, along with others from the Simon Wiesenthal Center, attended the ceremony.
Pictured left to right: a friend of the Wiesenthal Center; Martin Mendelson, counsel to
the Wiesenthal Center; me; then-President Bill Clinton; Rabbi Marvin Hier; First Lady
Hillary Clinton; Samuel Belzberg, founding chairman of the board of the Wiesenthal
Center; and rabbis Abraham Cooper and Meyer May, both deans of the Wiesenthal
Center.*

Top: The 38th President of the United States, Gerald Ford, between me and my beautiful wife, sometime in the 1970s. Right: In 1980, Simon was awarded the U.S. Congressional Gold Medal by President Jimmy Carter. Here I am at the ceremony with Walter Mondale, the vice president.

Top: Here we are with Al Gore, the 45th vice president of the United States.

Bottom: Senator Dodd and Simon attended the UJA South Shore Inaugural, where Joan and I were guests of honor.

Pictured left to right: My daughter Lynn, Senator Dodd, Joan, me, my daughter Nancy Rosen Stern, Simon, my daughter Ilene Rosen Cohen, and my son-in-law Larry Cohen.

Top: We met Margaret Thatcher, then the Prime Minister of the United Kingdom. Right: Because of my relationship with Simon and Rabbi Hier, Joan and I met Yitzhak Shamir, Israel's Prime Minister.

Talking with Henry Kissinger, former United States Secretary of State.

Shaking hands with Hussein bin Talal, then the King of Jordan.

Here I am pictured with Natan Sharansky, who was Chairman of the Executive for the Jewish Agency for Israel and is now chairman for the Institute for the Study of Global Antisemitism and Policy. In the 1970s and 1980s, Sharansky spent nearly a decade in Soviet prisons as refusenik, a term given to Soviet Jews who were denied permission to emigrate to Israel.

Because of Simon, I went twice to the White House with presidents of the United States. I made speeches to the Congressional committees. I was at the UN. I even met the Pope!

Rabbi Hier has a good relationship with Pope Francis, so in 2020, he invited the board, along with their spouses, to visit the Pope. The Pope sat and talked with us, and after it was over, he shook all our hands.

I said, "Your Holiness, I am very honored to be here with you today. When I was a very young man, I saw a lot of people killed in the war. I would hope that with your good wishes, they would stop the killing once and for all. Please make a special prayer for the state of Israel."

Look at the Pope's face! He's the sweetest man in the world.

HOLLYWOOD

B y and large, the world loved Simon. Hollywood in particular loved him because so many of them were Jewish, and they had an affinity for what the Simon Wiesenthal Center was doing.

Gregory Peck, Elizabeth Taylor, Kirk Douglas, Glenn Ford. Hollywood loved Simon because he was inspiring. We would hold fundraising dinners in at the Beverly Wilshire Hotel, the Century Plaza, and the Beverly-Hilton, and the dinners would be packed. President Bush came. It was incredible. We raised millions of dollars, and it was easy.

I remember that Joan was unable to attend one dinner, so Rabbi Hier called and asked if I would mind selling my ticket to someone else. I agreed, of course. When I arrived, a woman was sitting at the table with her back to me. She was the only person seated, so I sat next to her and introduced myself.

"Hello, my name is Martin Rosen."

She looked up and said, "Nice to meet you. I'm Barbara Streisand."

That was how it was with Simon. Celebrities would come out of the woodwork.

They paid their own way to these dinners because, to them, Simon was a rock star. Do not get me wrong: Simon never acted like a rock star, but in Hollywood, he was revered as much as any celebrity.

He took money only for his speeches, and even then, he charged half of what he was worth. He was a poor man who lived in an ordinary neighborhood and drove the same old, gray car for decades. Yet, he attracted people as if he was a legend—because he was. Simon was a legend.

Frank Sinatra more than anyone took a liking to Simon. At a dinner honoring Simon in 1980, Frank Sinatra, who was on the board of trustees of the Simon Wiesenthal Center, had this to say:

> *"You could not have selected an honoree I admire more and a man in whose name we gather tonight. I love Simon Wiesenthal with all my heart. I respect Simon Wiesenthal and I am proud to call him friend, and prouder still that he calls me friend.*
>
> *"His life has compensated for all of those lives who are wasted. His dedication to his fellow man stands as a very definition of the word. His courage is written boldly across our history as no other man has before in the history of the world.*
>
> *"His decency is engraved in our hearts where it remains a symbol of man's capability of loving his fellow man. Simon is more than his brother's keeper, much more, he is his friend's keeper, and more than that he is a stranger's keeper. And nowhere in the good book does God ask more of his children. I've met an army of good people as I've stumbled through life, but none whose call to arms rivals Mr. Wiesenthal's.*
>
> *"In conclusion of my own remarks, let me share with you this statement of truth, I would gladly give up every song*

I ever wrote to rest my head on the pillow of his accomplish-ments. I salute you. You are living proof that God knew what he was doing when he experimented making the rest of us until he perfected the image in you."

That is precisely how I feel: "I would gladly give up every song I ever wrote to rest my head on the pillow of his accomplishments."

Sinatra was a nice guy. People said he was a gangster. He was not. I became very friendly with Sinatra, and he stayed on our board until the day he died.

I was once at a very fancy restaurant in New York. As I was leaving, I saw Frank Sinatra sitting at a table. I walked toward his table, but the maître d' stepped in my way.

"Mr. Sinatra does not expect to be disturbed."

Then, I will never forget, Sinatra saw me, and he said, "Marty Rosen, how are you?"

Austrian-born Arnold Schwarzenegger, movie star and former governor of California, supported Simon as well. Top: Joan and I (both pictured with Schwarzenegger) met him at a fundraiser for the Simon Wiesenthal Center.

Bottom: Academy Award-winner Jon Voight standing between Simon and me.

Joan, Simon Wiesenthal, and Elizabeth Taylor, who was the world's highest-paid movie star in the 1960s and the member of the Simon Wiesenthal Center's board of trustees.

I went to Budapest for the filming of Murderers Among Us: the Simon Wiesenthal
Story. Top: Here I am with Academy Award-winning actor Ben Kingsley, who
played Simon Wiesenthal in the 1989 movie.
Bottom: Robert Cooper, Simon, and me. Cooper was the producer of Murderers
Among Us.

With Simon on the set of Murderers Among Us in Budapest.

My grandfather played a role in Simon's movie, I Have Never Forgotten You, *narrated by Nicole Kidman. When I graduated college, I collaborated with the Wiesenthal Center to a host a cocktail party to debut the movie to my friends and young professionals. My grandfather spoke, and as he always does, he spoke eloquently without notes. People were amazed at his story, his relationship with Simon, and what they were able to achieve.*

David and I know how important the Wiesenthal Center is to my grandfather, and we are going to continue that legacy.

—Bari Cohen Klein, our granddaughter

RESTING HIS HEAD

Shortly before Simon died, he called me at home on a Sunday night. I was planning to fly to Europe the next day to take two of my grandchildren to Europe for their Bar Mitzvahs, which had always been my tradition. "Marty, I want to see you before I die," Simon said to me.

He was in his nineties, and so I said, "I will fly out tonight."

I bought a one-way ticket to Vienna, and I boarded the plane with no luggage. I flew to Vienna and spent six hours with my dear, dear friend. While I was there, I told him that I had three important questions for him.

"Number One: Where do you want to be buried?" I knew from his daughter that Simon would not answer that question. I guess he thought that all the dying he had seen in his life was evil, and he did not want to talk about losing his life.

He was annoyed, but he told me he wanted to be buried in Tel Aviv.

"Number Two: What do you want to be done with your papers?" This was a matter of honor, and he wanted to ship the papers to the Museum of Tolerance in Los Angeles.

I asked him my third question, and he answered.

I said goodbye to him. I knew I would not see my brother again.

After I left, I walked to the center of Vienna and wrote his obituary, which I put in my pocket. Jewish people get buried quickly, and I wanted to put my obituary for Simon in the paper right away.

Simon died shortly after I returned from my trip to Europe, resting his head for the final time on his mighty pillow of accomplishments. His daughter, Paulinka, called me at 2:30 in the morning. She asked me to come to the funeral in Israelto give the family eulogy.

Eight heads of state and I gave eulogies that day, September 23, 2005. After I gave my speech, the chief rabbi of Israel said to me, "Mr. Rosen, your speech was the best because you did not read it."

It is true. I did not read my speech. I gave my speech.

Simon's funeral was on a Friday. We stayed in Tel Aviv on Saturday for the Jewish holiday, and on Sunday, I fulfilled Simon's final request of me.

When he was dying, I asked three questions. That third question was: "What would you like me to do with the money that I have raised for you over the years?"

On that day, the Sunday after his death, I told my wife that I had to do one last thing for Simon. We took a car from Tel Aviv to Jerusalem, where the Hebrew University is located.

I went to the front desk of the Hebrew University.

"I would like to see the president of the college."

"Do you have an appointment?"

"No."

"Why do you want to see him?"

"I have money for him."

I had decided that when Simon died, I would stop raising money. I took what I had saved in my own bank and donated it to the foundation, dedicating a scholarship in perpetuity in Simon's name to needy students who study the Holocaust.

And that marked the end of my story with Simon. He was the greatest man I ever knew.

THE EULOGY FOR MY BROTHER, SIMON

Paulinka, Gerard, grandchildren, and friends: It is a great honor for me to say a few words about my dear, dear friend, Simon Wiesenthal, at this time. We all know that Simon was one of the great men of the twentieth century. He was a man amongst men who made a statement with his life. He will be remembered long past the time when many others with diverse credentials will be remembered. He proved that one person can make a difference if they really try. It is often said that in this large, cruel, unusual world you can't rock the system. He did. He did it by himself, lonely at times, with little support, economic and otherwise, but he did it by himself, and he pursued the cause of justice for the six million Jews and countless millions of others who were murdered by the Nazi criminals.

It was a most unusual union and set of circumstances that Simon and I became acquainted, particularly in view of our very diverse backgrounds. I was born in New York and at eighteen went to war. I had the grim opportunity to view some of the camps when I was nineteen years old. American soldiers were not really prepared to see the things that we saw and encountered. Then, in 1965, some twenty years after the war, I had the great privilege of meeting this most unusual and dynamic man. For forty years, we had been close friends and associates. This man who I have known so well visited my home in Long Island on many occasions.

I have three daughters, and he often rendered his opinion on their male friends. Simon was a man always possessed of opinions, and most of the time they were thought out and correct. In the last years he would particularly revel in lecturing to young people knowing that they are the future, and it was most imperative that they understood what occurred. He also lectured German youth and knew full well that the sins of the father should not fall on the children.

It was interesting to point out that one day in 1977 Simon called me and said that some young Rabbi had visited him in Vienna and wanted to establish a holocaust center in the North American hemisphere. Simon thought that it would be a good idea the next time I went to California to visit with him and to evaluate it and to make my recommendations to Simon. I met with Rabbi Hier in California, and I immediately knew that this was a winning combination. Simon Wiesenthal and Rabbi Hier and thus the Simon Wiesenthal Center was established and has become a respected worldwide major Jewish organization. It will provide the perpetuity of Simon's life and work which is so important for the world and the future of all people.

Through the years there have been some detractors of Simon; the people who thought the holocaust belonged to them. Indeed, the holocaust belonged to no one, and it belonged to everyone. Simon, indeed, was the only one who, throughout all the years, lonely at times, out of funds, out of moral and actual support, but he kept it alive. Had he not kept it alive, there would be no discussion of Nazi hunting in the last 25 years. When the statute of limitations was set to expire in West Germany on December 31, 1979, it was through the work of

Simon and the people of the Wiesenthal Center in lobbying the West German government to abolish the statute of limitations forever and, therefore, the cause continues through this very day.

Dear, dear Simon: it is time to say goodbye. But before I do, I would like to tell you about a passage in Simon's last book Justice Not Vengeance, which is contained in the foreword to the book, where Simon pays tribute to the people that have helped him along the way. I quote: "Thanks to the flow of money from the JDC, we were able to conduct a series of costly investigations overseas, investigations which would probably have been impossible otherwise. From New York also came those seven thousand dollars which I had to pay for information on the whereabouts of the commandant of Treblinka, Franz Stangl. Herman Katz died in 1977 and his attorney and co-founder of the New York office, Martin Rosen, took over his function. As my family was exterminated by the Nazis, and as I have scarcely any relations left, I once said to Martin how nice it would be if one could choose a new family for oneself—in which case I would choose him as a brother. Thus we became brothers."

So dear brother Simon, rest in peace. Your job was well done. We and the entire world will always remember you. You made a difference.

A PATRIOT

────────────

When Nancy was eighteen and the other girls were away at school, my wife and I decided to take Nancy to Spain. One day, we were sitting in a town on the Spanish Riviera having a drink, and at the next table were two couples about our age. I said, "Look at them. They are Jewish, too."

Nancy said, "Shhh, Daddy."

I said, "No, no. There's nothing wrong with being Jewish."

And then I loudly called out, "Landsman!"

Landsman is a Yiddish word that means, "You are like my brother!"

The two Jewish couples sitting next to us took notice and brought over their chairs. They told us where they were from: Leeds and Birmingham, both in England.

We went on to exchange our experiences of being Jewish from different parts of the world. And for three days, we continued to have dinner.

On the third day, when it was time to say goodbye, one of them asked me, "Are you Jewish first, or are you American first?"

It was a very good question. No one had asked me that before.

"It's very easy," I said. "I am first an American because only in America can I be as good of a Jew as I am."

At all home games, between the top and the bottom of the seventh inning, when the Yankees are due to come up, the New York Yankees stand to sing God Bless America with their hand where it belongs—on their heart. New Yorkers have a great allegiance to the United Sates, so they also honor a veteran.

On August 3, 2022, the Yankees played the Seattle Mariners. I was the veteran honoree, standing before about 30,000 people when the announcer called my name: Staff Sergeant Martin Rosen of Hewlett.

A number of my family and friends were at that game—some of them didn't even know I was being honored, so they were surprised. I took the whole family, and we filled eighteen seats.

It was a good day, and a great honor.

He is very patriotic. He remembers his America, and he is a proud veteran. I remember when he was going to vote, he wore his World War II veteran hat, and strangers came and thanked him for his service. It was amazing to see. I didn't think people were that patriotic anymore, but strangers kept coming up to him and thanking him. We were standing in line to vote, and people just parted the sea for him and said, "Go ahead of us."

This past summer, the New York Yankees honored my dad as the veteran of the game. He grew up a poor boy in the Bronx, and he loved the Yankees. He remembers paying $1 to go see the Yankees. The amount of patriotism at the game was overwhelming. He loved that day.

—Ilene Rosen Cohen, our oldest daughter

My dad is probably the most patriotic person I know.

We grew up having dinner with Simon Wiesenthal and hearing stories about the Holocaust. Being Jewish was important to my father.

We went to an Orthodox temple as kids, and my mom and sisters and I sat separately. My father sat alone because we were all girls. But it never felt forced. The feeling that I got out of it was that Judaism binds us as a family.

—Lynn Rosen Karkus, our middle daughter

In the full circle of life, my oldest son, Eli, who is four, recently learned the story of Passover, Jewish persecution and what it "means" to be Jewish. He started to inquire about the people in his life, wondering if they were Jewish or not. I loved being able to tell him that Papa Marty, out of all the people in the world we knew, was the one person that was the proudest to be Jewish.

Just being privileged to have had all this time with him so that my children have gotten to know him so well, love him, and learn from him has been the biggest blessing of all.

—Kerri Cohen Saperstein, our granddaughter

ACKNOWLEDGEMENTS

I would like to thank my wife for marrying me. On more than one occasion, I have been the guest of honor, but without a doubt, the highest honor of all has been walking through life as Joan's husband.

Joan and I never did have a son, but we had something much better: We had three wonderful daughters, each of whom married a great man who became like a son. Ilene and Larry, Lynn and Ted, Nancy, and Steven: You have given us eight grandchildren and seven great-grandchildren—Bari, Kerri, Andrew, Michael, Corey, Jason, Samantha, and Brett, and Tyler, Eli, Emma, Cole, Aiden, Asher, and Arielle (with more on the way). I hope that when they read this book, they are as proud of me as I am of them, of you, and of our family.

It would be remiss to not mention the many people who have contributed to my life, including my many relatives, the men who served with me in the Army, my work colleagues, my clients, my friends, and the heroes who helped Simon fight war crimes. That said, the list—like my life—would be long, and I fear I would erroneously exclude someone of great importance to me. I have gone as far as I can. I had a very full life. I really have no regrets in anything I did, so if you are reading this book, you (or someone you love) have likely contributed to this great run of mine. Thank you, and God bless.

The New Y

VOL.CXXXV.... No. 46,666   Copyright © 1986 The New York Times   *NEW YORK, SUND.*

By LAWRENCE VAN GELDER

Eye on Taxes and c

The New York Times / Nancy Kaye

Martin Rosen

"NOTHING is going to happen until well into 1986, which makes it chaotic."

In the offices of Rosen & Reade at 666 Fifth Avenue in Manhattan, Martin Rosen of Hewlett Harbor was delivering an assessment of the atmosphere created by the failure of Congress to pass a tax-revision bill after months of proposals and debate last year.

"Some part of this bill," he said, "will affect every individual in the country and every corporation."

The 60-year-old Mr. Rosen is not only a lawyer who is the founder and a senior partner of the 25-lawyer firm that bears his name, but also a certified public accountant and partner in the accounting firm of Martin Rosen & Company, which has 50 employees.

For much of the last year, as lawyer and accountant, he has been studying the various tax bills before Congress — the latest being a document of more than a thousand pages. And while it seems likely that current tax laws will be revised, no new law has been passed. "So," Mr. Rosen asked, "how can business people who are our clients and lawyers like ourselves plan their affairs if we don't know what the law is going to be?"

Nevertheless, he said, it is possible to regard the current proposals as

LONG ISLANDERS

embodying the limits of any new law and to tell clients: "If you can live with this, proceed with what you propose to do. If you can't, wait till we have definitive legislation."

But for Mr. Rosen, who also has lectured for many years on estate planning in courses for lawyers expanding their expertise at the Practising Law Institute in Manhattan, there is more to life than tax law and balance sheets.

For the last 20 years, Mr. Rosen has

This article ran in the New York Times *on Super Bowl Sunday: January 26, 1986.*

ork Times

Late Edition

Weather: Rainy and breezy today; southeasterly winds. Showers tonight. Showers or flurries likely tomorrow. Temperatures: today 45-50, tonight 36-40; yesterday 28-45. Details on page 23.

)AY, JANUARY 26, 1986

$1.50 beyond 75 miles from New York City, except on Long Island.

$1.2

on History's Lessons

acted without fee as the attorney for Simon Weisenthal, the hunter of Nazi war criminals. He is also a member of the board of trustees of the Simon Weisenthal Center in Los Angeles, the largest Holocaust study center in the United States. In addition, Mr. Rosen is president of the Jewish Documentation Center, which supports Mr. Weisenthal's work.

In 1979, Mr. Rosen was part of a 12-member group that journeyed to Bonn to meet with the West German Chancellor and leading members of the Bundestag to press the case for abolishing the German statute of limitations on German war crimes. Shortly thereafter, the statute was abolished.

Mr. Rosen, married, a father of three and a former Mayor of Lawrence, has also devoted some of his time to lecturing young people about the Holocaust, especially on Long Island, where he is a member of the South Shore executive committee of the United Jewish Appeal-Federation of Jewish Philanthropies campaign.

"I want to get the message through," he said of his Holocaust lectures. "Basically they've got to know what happened so it won't happen again. Remember, 40 years have passed, and many people are putting it on the back burner. We feel it's important for young people, Jewish and non-Jewish, to know that man's inhumanity to man happened in the 20th century. This is not the crusades. This is the 20th century."

Mr. Rosen came to his career and to his concern for others from a childhood in the Bronx. After graduation from DeWitt Clinton High School in 1942, he entered City College and studied accounting for a year before spending three years as a combat engineer in Europe and the South Pacific during World War II. When he returned to civilian life in 1946, he earned a bachelor's degree in business administration but had already decided to become a lawyer.

He worked for two years as an accountant and began to study at night at the New York University Law School, which awarded him a bachelor of laws degree in 1952.

By then he had already been conducting corporate income-tax investigations for two years for the Internal Revenue Service. While he was studying for his master's degree in law and taxation at N.Y.U., he became a certified public accountant and a partner in an accounting firm.

"And then around 1956," he said, "I decided to go into my own practice as both a lawyer and an accountant. The tax field changes more than probably all the fields of law together. It's a very challenging and complex field of endeavor."

Mr. Rosen traces his involvement in Jewish affairs to his late father, Irving, a Russian immigrant who was an ardent Zionist.

"He gave whatever he could or raised whatever he could for Israel," Mr. Rosen said, "before it became a state and when it became a state."

"Jews," he added, "must support their brethren."